"But What About Socialization?"

Answering the Perpetual Home Schooling Question

A Review of the Literature

Susan A. McDowell, Ed.D.

Philodeus Press
Nashville, Tennessee

"But What About Socialization"?
Answering the Perpetual Home Schooling Question
A Review of the Literature

Copyright © 2004

by Susan A. McDowell
All Rights Reserved

Published by:
Philodeus Press
P.O. Box 148351
Nashville, TN 37214-8351 U.SA.
World Wide Web Site: http://www.philodeuspress.com
e-mail: philodeuspress@earthlink.net

Library of Congress Control Number: 2003097308
International Standard Book Number (ISBN): 0-9744078-0-1
Printed by Morris Publishing, 3212 East Highway 30,
Kearney, NE 68847

Acknowledgments

I am eternally grateful for the countless blessings I have in my life, blessings that include many helpful, loving, and supportive family members and friends. I am especially grateful for the wisdom, guidance, unconditional love, prayers, and support of my husband, Stephen McDowell, my mother, Dr. Lovelle Atkisson, my sister, Laurie Britt, and my nephew, Scott Britt. These are not only my closest family members, but they are also my closest, dearest friends and trusted prayer partners.

To my treasured friend of a lifetime, Agnes Hooper, I give a heartfelt "thanks" for the many years of solid, enduring, and priceless friendship.

And many thanks to the wonderfully talented Andie Roberts, whose insights into the many idiosyncrasies of my software program saved me not only countless hours, but also countless headaches.

To my mentors in home schooling research – Dr. Brian Ray and Dr. Robert Crowson – I offer my sincere gratitude for the knowledge, the guidance, and, most especially, the friendship.

And, finally, and most importantly of all, I want to give thanks and praise to the Lord my God, His son, Jesus Christ, and the Holy Spirit, Who has forgiven me, saved me, healed me in both body and soul, set my feet on a solid rock, blessed me with more than I could ask or think, and given me a peace and joy in my life that I never thought possible. Thank You my Father, my Savior, my Provider, my Defender, and my Friend.

A very special thank you to our very special friend,

Michael McAlister

About the Author

Dr. Susan A. McDowell (Ed.D) received her doctorate in education from Vanderbilt University in 1998. She is the author of several published articles on home schooling, and has conducted research into many of the differing facets of the home schooling movement, including the role of the mother-teacher, socialization, the participation and perception of minorities in home schooling, home schooling in the political arena, and home schooling as an epidemiological phenomenon. She is the Editor of the *Home School Researcher* (the academic, refereed journal of the National Home Education Research Institute), and is the co-editor of a special, two-part issue of the refereed *Peabody Journal of Education*, entitled *The Home Education Movement in Context, Practice, and Theory* (2000).

Dr. McDowell has presented research concerning home schooling and the home schooling movement at multiple national educational conferences, and has been interviewed regarding her research on both radio and television. She has also been interviewed for a number of national publications, including *Education Week, The Boston Globe*, and *The Wall Street Journal*. She and her husband make their very happy home in Nashville, TN.

Table of Contents

Introduction

As an educational movement, home schooling continues to experience phenomenal growth. Currently, an estimated 1.5 to 2.0 million children are home schooled in the United States.[1] Research on the academic achievement and social adjustment of home schooled children abounds, as well as research presenting the beliefs, practices, socioeconomic levels, educational background, and ethnicity of home schooling parents. Although some voices have offered negative commentaries on the practice of home schooling,[2] research studies indicate that home schooled students perform well in terms of both academic achievement[3] and social and psychological development.[4] Home education is thriving; its ranks are swelling, and its children – according to the most current research – are flourishing.

Given these firmly established facts, one cannot help but wonder why the "socialization question" continues to arise with such perplexing consistency. But it does. "But what about socialization?" is a question that seems to pop up everywhere and from almost everybody at some time or another. I'm embarrassed to admit that I even asked it myself 12 years ago when my younger sister informed me that she had decided to home school her son.

Since this question is such a persistent one, and since the home schooling movement is increasing in both number and acceptability, I believe that there is a genuine need for a book that deals with this issue exclusively. Home schoolers are a very research-literate, educated population, and so they are keenly aware of the fact that the research exists that vindicates their educational choice in matters of socialization. However, a book like this one that pulls together all of the research related to this issue simply didn't exist, until now.

It is the purpose of this book, then, to provide in one place as much pertinent information as possible relevant to the issue of socialization in home schooling. In an effort to present an effective compilation/synthesis of the material, I have endeavored to let the home schoolers and the researchers "speak" for themselves as much as possible, without inserting myself unnecessarily between what they had to say and the reader.

First, of course, it was necessary to clarify what is meant by the term "socialization," as well as to explore the different meanings different people may have when asking the same question. This subject is explored in Chapter I ("Just What *Is* Socialization?").

In order to tackle this issue in a manner both thorough and practical, the second chapter is devoted to the real experts in dealing with this question -- the home schoolers themselves. In Chapter II ("Voices From the Front"), real home schoolers are cited at length concerning their feelings about and approaches to this issue. Information was drawn from a variety of sources, including the internet and home schooling publications.

Chapter III ("What Does the Research Have to Say?") is devoted to the research studies that have investigated this matter. Where possible, the actual abstract from the research study is provided, along with discussions of the study's methodology and findings.

In Chapter IV ("Yes, But Doesn't the NEA Have Some Negative Things to Say About Home Schooling?"), the NEA's position -- and the possible reasons for that position -- are explored and examined.

Finally, the concluding chapter ("Conclusion: This Question Can Be Put to Rest") does just that. Taking into consideration all the information and research provided in the preceding chapters, an altogether positive conclusion is unavoidable. "A Special Message From the Author to Home Schoolers"-- which deals with the importance of research -- closes the chapter.

Also included, as an Appendix, is a small research study I conducted on home schoolers' perceptions of the socialization issue. Finally, rounding out the text is a "Suggested Bibliography." It is my genuine hope that this book serves a real and positive purpose in the home schooling community, and that it fills a void in the home schooling literature. It is also my hope that the home schooling movement itself continues to grow in terms of size, recognition, and political power -- a sure testimony to the character, commitment, determination, and dedication of home schooling parents everywhere.

Endnotes -- Introduction

[1] Ray, B. D. (2002). *A quick reference worldwide guide to home-schooling: Facts and stats on the benefits of home school, 2002, 2003.* Nashville, TN: Broadman & Holman.

[2] Apple, M. W. (2000). The cultural politics of home schooling. *Peabody Journal of Education, 75* (1 & 2), 256-271.
See also the following:
Lubienski, C. (2000). Whither the common good? A critique of home schooling. *Peabody Journal of Education, 75* (1 & 2), 207-232.
National Education Association. (1990). *The 1990-91 resolutions of the National Education Association.* Washington, DC: Author.

[3] Ray, B. D. (1997). *Strengths of their own – Home schoolers across America: Academic achievement, family characteristics, and longitudinal traits.* Salem, OR: National Home Education Research Institute.
See also the following:
Ray, B. D. (1999). *Home schooling on the threshold: A survey of research at the dawn of the new millennium.* Salem, OR: National Home Education Research Institute.
Ray, B. D. (2000). Home schooling: The ameliorater of negative influences on learning? *Peabody Journal of Education, 75* (1 & 2), 71-106.

Rudner, L. M. (1999). Scholastic achievement and demographic characteristics of homes school students in 1998. *Education Policy Analysis Archives, 7* (8) [electronic journal], available online at: http://epaa.asu.edu/epaa/v7n8
Wartes, J. (1988, June). Summary of two reports from the Washington Home School Research Project, 1987. *Home School Researcher, 5* (2), 1-4.

4 Kelley, S. W. (1991). Socialization of home schooled children: A self-concept study. *Home School Researcher, 7* (4) 1-12.
See also the following:
Medlin, R. G. (2000). Home schooling and the question of socialization. *Peabody Journal of Education, 75* (1 & 2), 207-232.
Shyers, L. E. (1992). A comparison of social adjustment between home and traditionally schooled students. *Home School Researcher, 8* (3), 1-8.

Chapter I

Just What **Is** *Socialization?*

This is a highly logical question with, perhaps unfortunately, more than one correct answer. Usually found in the dictionary under the heading "socialize," it means, according to *The Random House College Dictionary*, "to make social; make fit for life in companionship with others; to make socialistic; establish or regulate according to the theories of socialism; to treat as a group activity; to associate or mingle sociably with others."[1] (Clearly, that particular part of the definition having to do with socialism as a political movement does not apply to this discussion.)

And what do other sources have to say on the subject? Definitions found on the Internet offer a variety of meanings. For example, the *On-line Medical Dictionary* sees socialization as "the training or molding of an individual through various relationships, educational agencies, and social controls, which enables him to become a member of a particular society."[2] *Dictionary.com* offers several definitions from different sources, including: "1. To place under government or group ownership or control. 2. To make fit for companionship with others; make sociable. 3. To convert or adapt to the needs of society. 4. To take part in social activities." (from *The American Heritage Dictionary of the English Language*, 4th ed.), and from *Princeton University's WordNet*: "1. The act of meeting for social purposes; 'there was too much socialization with the enlisted men.' 2. The adoption of the behavior patterns of the surrounding culture."[3]

Such definitions are helpful as a starting point for a general understanding of what is involved in the issue of socialization. However, what is meant by the asker of the question "But what about socialization?" may differ substantially from person to person. In fact, it is for this very reason that Professor Richard G. Medlin -- in his article on home schooling and socialization -- called this same question "the most familiar and the most puzzling" that home schoolers face.[4] As Medlin so aptly points out,

> "What makes this question so puzzling is that different people mean different things by the word *socialization*. Some people mean social activity: giving children the chance to play with friends and participate in traditional extracurricular activities like sports, school plays, and the senior prom. Others mean influence: teaching children to conform to majority norms. And some mean social exposure: introducing children to the culture and values of different groups of people."[5]

In order to address all the potentially different shades of meaning wrapped up in this one question, Medlin suggests that the question itself be

> "recast into three more specific questions that are consistent with an accurate definition of socialization: Do home-schooled children participate in the daily routines of their communities? Are they acquiring the rules of behavior and systems of beliefs and attitudes they need? Can they function effectively as members of society?"[6]

As an educational researcher, I am very happy to able to inform you that the short answer to all of these questions is "yes." The details of the research that allows me to state this with such complete confidence are found in the chapters that follow.

Endnotes - Chapter I

1 (p. 1247). Stein, J. (Ed). (1984). *The Random House college dictionary* (rev. ed.). New York: Random House.

2 On-line Medical Dictionary. (2001). Available at: http://www.graylab.ac.uk/cgi-bin/omd?/socialization (retrieved 7/3/01).

3 Dictionary.com. (2001). Available online at: http://www.dictionary.com/cgi/dict.pl?term=socialization (retrieved 7/3/01).

4 (p. 107). Medlin, R. G.. (2000). Home schooling and the question of socialization. In S. A. McDowell & B. D. Ray (Eds.), *The home education movement in context, practice, and theory* (pp. 107-123). *Peabody Journal of Education, 75* (1 & 2).

5 (p. 107). Medlin, R. G.. (2000). Home schooling and the question of socialization. In S. A. McDowell & B. D. Ray (Eds.), *The home education movement in context, practice, and theory* (pp. 107-123). *Peabody Journal of Education, 75* (1 & 2).

6 (p. 110). Medlin, R. G.. (2000). Home schooling and the question of socialization. In S. A. McDowell & B. D. Ray (Eds.), *The home education movement in context, practice, and theory* (pp. 107-123). *Peabody Journal of Education, 75* (1 & 2).

Chapter II

Voices From the Front

Hearing the Voices From the Front: What Home Schooling Parents, Authors, Leaders, and Home Schooled Children Have to Say About Socialization

Who are the *real* experts on socialization and home schooling? Home schoolers, of course. They're the ones who have dealt with this issue on an ongoing basis for quite some time, and, not surprisingly, they have a great deal to say about the subject. In this chapter, we'll hear from a wide variety of experts -- including home schooling parents, authors, and leaders in the movement—and from some home schooled children as well.

Hearing From: Home Schooling Parents

Mary Griffith--in *The Homeschooling Handbook* (1997)–paints the following lighthearted picture of some home schoolers' response to the socialization question:

> "Homeschooling skeptics will often concede that academics are seldom a problem for homeschoolers, but they'll always come through with 'But what about socialization?' This question is so common that many experienced homeschoolers can hardly restrain themselves from spluttering or giggling whenever they hear someone start to ask it, and they'll often finish the

question and be halfway through a detailed response before the questioner can take a breath."[1]

One home schooling parent, Gwen Meehan, has her own thoughtful and thought-provoking response:

"The first question we are always asked is about Pat's 'socialization.' I respond by asking them to go back to their own schooling and see if they were really happy with their own socialization. I suggest that even if they were the most popular person in the school, if they will look at that experience honestly, they'll recognize that it was not a wholly positive experience. (The most popular/beautiful/talented person in the school is hated behind their [sic] back and they know it surely). No one has ever disagreed with me. Rather, people are most often shocked that they had never stopped to look at that part of their life realistically before."[2]

And from "The Canon Family's Homeschool Homepage," we have a slightly different take on this persistent question:

"What about socialization? This is the most often asked question and concern. People often seem to think that homeschooling occurs in a vacuum whereas it really happens in the world at large. Children learn social skills by modeling what they see and hear. Would you rather your child take her cues from the librarian, the kids in Sunday school, and the woman at the museum or from a group of twenty same-age peers? Of course children need social exposure and homeschoolers need to provide that. They do so through scouting, enrichment activities, neighborhood kids and homeschool groups. Children who attend public school may appear more social than some homeschooled children but if you look at social skills you will usually find that the home-educated child has a distinct advantage."[3]

Carol is a California home schooling mother who has her own very valid reasons for preferring the socialization that home schooling can offer:

"My primary reason for homeschooling is socialization. I want to let each of my children live, grow, and decide for herself who she is and what her beliefs are. I believe that the structure of school effectively prevents this, pure and simple . . . I have many other reasons, some selfish. I love my kids, didn't come by them easily in either case, and enjoy their company. I want our family to decide the schedule we use . . . if we want one at all. I want to respect that Shauna is in a coma at 8:00 a.m., but fresh and alert at 10:00 p.m. I want Rosalie, who fatigues easily when reading (because of her corneal scarring), to read in short bits, when it fits for her. .... I love seeing my kids find amazing, inventive answers to real life needs. To solve problems, both create things that they wouldn't have thought of if someone had rushed in with 'the way everyone else does it.'"[4]

According to Tammy, a home schooling Mom from Texas,

"The homeschooling setting is ideal for socialization. In classroom settings, children are locked away for eight hours a day with thirty or so of their peers and, as a result, are deprived of the chance to interact with those outside their own age group. The homeschooling setting, on the other hand, provides the child with opportunities to interact with people of all ages, occupations, and interests, which tends to result in well-rounded, sociable, confident individuals."[5]

And, to Californian home schooling mother Pam,

> "Socialization is, really and truly, a complete non-issue.
> People worry about it and they shouldn't. Not even a
> little bit. Unless you lock your children in the basement,
> they will get 'socialized.' There are so many
> opportunities that I cannot even fathom considering
> school as one of them: Scouts, church groups, 4-H,
> various classes, neighborhood kids–the list is endless.
> And, as I always say, 'Oh, socialization? Yes, we're *very*
> concerned about that – that's why our kids don't go to
> school!'"[6]

Shari (a home schooling mother in Alabama) handles the "S"
question this way:

> "We're very well socialized, thank you. I think kids,
> generally speaking, are bad for other kids. They may
> like each other, but they like chocolate, and I wouldn't let
> them eat all they wanted. Between swimming,
> neighbors, dance, Sunday School – well, they've got
> enough of what the world calls socialization."[7]

Given the number of personal home schooling web sites on
the internet, it is clear that home schoolers are a very computer
savvy and internet-wise bunch. Heather Madrone uses her own
website to discuss the socialization issue in great depth:

> "I was reading the mini-flame war about homeschooling
> over in misc.kids and someone trotted the socialization
> bugaboo out again. I've always felt vaguely
> uncomfortable when someone asks about socialization. I
> realized that I'd never heard the word before I started
> homeschooling and that I didn't really know what it
> meant.
> So I decided to look it up.

I found it under the word 'socialize.' Here's the definition:

1. To place under government or group ownership or control; establish on a socialistic basis.
2. To fit for companionship with others; make sociable in attitude or manners.
3. To convert or adapt to the needs of society.
4. To take part in social activities.

I was thrown by definition #1. Do we really want children to be owned or controlled by the government? To be socialized like medicine or railroads? I assume this is *not* what people mean when they talk about homeschooled youngsters receiving insufficient socialization, but I could be wrong.

If definition #1 is what people mean by socialization, then I'm afraid homeschooled children aren't going to be nearly as socialized as public schooled youngsters. Actually, I'd be more afraid of the people who want to socialize children in such a fashion. When I read definition #1, a chill went down my spine. Definition #3 bothered me too, seeming more suited to institutions than human beings.

Definitions 2 and 4 don't bother me at all. I'd like my children to be fit companions for other people. I'd like them to have manners and treat other people courteously and in a friendly manner. I want them to take part in social activities, to enjoy being part of the community.

I just don't see how children need to go to school to accomplish definitions 2 and 4.

So, someone tell me, please, what is this property of 'socialization' and how it is conferred by the schools and not in any other way?

I know this topic comes up over and over again, but it's really bothering me now. I think that part of what may be meant by socialization *is* definitions 1 and 3, that people want our children to become good cogs in the machine, mindless members of the mass culture.

Forgive my melodrama. When I think of children who are taught to blindly obey authority and to fit in, I think of the horrors of Nazi Germany and the Stalin regime. I don't want to see that happen in this country."[8]

Hearing From: Home Schooling Authors

There are a great many excellent books and articles about home schooling in print at this point in time. Some of these books were written by home schooling parents themselves-- books in which these parents share their personal insights and experiences about the home schooling process and the socialization question--and others were written by educators and/or researchers.

One of the earliest outspoken advocates for home schooling was John Holt who, in his 1981 book, *Teach Your Own: A Hopeful Path for Education*, had the following to say about the socialization issue:

"If there were no other reason for wanting to keep kids out of school, the social life would be reason enough. In all but a very few of the schools I have taught in, visited, or know anything about, the social life of the children is mean-spirited, competitive, exclusive, status-seeking, snobbish, full of talk about who went to whose birthday party and who got what Christmas presents and who got how many Valentine cards and who is talking to so-and-so and who is not. Even in the first grade, classes soon divide up into leaders (energetic and–often deservedly-popular kids), their bands of followers, and other outsiders who are pointedly excluded from these groups. I remember my sister saying of one of her children, then five, that she never knew her to do anything really mean or silly until she went away to school -- a nice school, by the way, in a nice small town.

Jud Jerome, writer, poet, former professor at Antioch, wrote about his son, Topher, meeting this so-called 'social life' in a free school run by a commune:

.... Though we were glad he was happy and enjoying himself (in school), we were also sad as we watched him deteriorate from a person into a kid under peer influence in school. It was much like what we saw happening when he was in kindergarten. There are certain kinds of childishness which it seems most people accept as being natural, something children have to go through, something which it is, indeed, a shame to deny them. Silliness, self-indulgence, random rebelliousness, secretiveness, cruelty to other children, clubbishness, addiction to toys, possessions, junk, spending money, purchased entertainment, exploitation of adults to pay attention, take them places, amuse them, do things with them -- all these things seem to me quite unnecessary, not 'normal' at all (note: except in the sense of being common), and just as disgusting in children as they are in adults. And while they develop as a result of peer influence, I believe this is only and specifically because children are thrown together in school and develop these means, as prisoners develop means of passing dull time and tormenting authorities to cope with an oppressive situation. The richer the families the children come from, the worse these traits seem to be. Two years of school and Topher would probably have regressed two years in emotional development. I am not sure of that, of course, and it was not because of that fear that we pulled him out, but we saw enough of what happened to him in a school situation not to regret pulling him out."[9]

Clearly, this is the sort of environment that Mayberry, Knowles, Ray, and Marlow had in mind when they noted in *Home Schooling: Parents as Educators* (1995), that:

"Opponents of home education frequently voice a concern about the social development of children educated at home. They argue that interaction with other children is a vital part of formal schooling that cannot be addressed in the home. Home school parents, on the other hand, often claim that the current social environment of formal schools is a compelling argument for operating a home school."[10]

Another educational researcher, Richard Medlin, provides an illuminating overview of the research on this issue in his article, "Home Schooling and the Question of Socialization," in which he concludes that

"although there are still far too many unanswered questions about home schooling and socialization, some preliminary conclusions can be stated. Home-schooled children are taking part in the daily routines of their communities. They are certainly not isolated; in fact, they associate with—and feel close to—all sorts of people. Home schooling parents can take much of the credit for this. For, with their children's long-term social development in mind, they actively encourage their children to take advantage of social opportunities outside the family. Home-schooled children are acquiring the rules of behavior and systems of beliefs and attitudes they need. They have good self-esteem and are likely to display fewer behavior problems than do other children. They may be more socially mature and have better leadership skills than other children as well. And they appear to be functioning effectively as members of adult society."[11]

David Guterson is a home schooling parent who took the time to write the very helpful and now-familiar classic, *Family Matters: Why Homeschooling Makes Sense* (1992). In this work, Guterson explores the socialization question in great detail:

"But what about your children's socialization is a question I am far more likely to field than *How well are they learning?* It is also a far more perplexing question, chiefly because there are many definitions of a proper socialization but also because objective measures of socialization, however defined, are of dubious value at best. No one really knows what socialization is or how to identify it in the lives of children -- homeschooled children and all others. Despite the best efforts of sociologists and anthropologists, authoritative answers to common questions about socialization elude schoolers and homeschoolers both. *But what about your children's socialization?* is a riddle that ought to perplex every parent. "

Noting that different people mean different things by the same question, Guterson elaborates further, explaining that "the question is often posed to me by people with something very clear in mind: maintaining our fragile social consensus."

In detailing more of the different meanings behind the same question, Guterson points out that

"For others, the question is a far less idealistic one, aimed not at the cohesiveness of society but at the competitive social advantage of individuals. Here, *What about your children's socialization?* means, in essence, *How do you expect them to understand people well enough to get ahead in the world if you don't send them to school?.* ....
But *what about your sons' socialization?* is for others among our schooling friends a question about their current social life. .... For others the socialization question is about whether Robin and I can accept the inevitability of our sons' movement away from us. Here, *What about your sons' socialization?* means *What about weaning yourselves from them and allowing them to make their own path through life?* .... Finally there is the set of social realists who ask, *But what about your sons' socialization?*

and mean by it that life in a mass society requires--for better or worse--a mass form of socialization at school."[12]

Clearly, Guterson is a very keen and thoughtful observer of the place the socialization question has taken in the life of the home schooling parent.

Cheryl Gorder, in *Home Schools: An Alternative*, articulates her take on the issue with the following highly detailed statement:

> "One of the most frequent criticisms of home schools by people who have preconceived notions about the subject is that they believe that these children are missing out socially. Over 80% of the educators I surveyed felt that home schools were at a disadvantage in the social development of the child, and 59% felt that a disadvantage of home schools was the lack of competition in the child's academic and social world. Educators were vehement in their support of schools as a social tool. One teacher stated:
>
> 'A child at home is isolated. It [home schooling] is unrealistic. It might seem fine now, but what will happen when these kids get out into the real world and Mom's not around any more? It's almost like putting up a glass house and saying nothing bad will ever happen. She [the home schooled child] is going to miss interaction with other students. I don't know how to say this diplomatically, but I do not think home schooling is appropriate for any children. It's a serious responsibility that the parent must recognize.'"

Gorder continues her examination of the issue with the following observations, pointing out that:

"The teachers and administrators who dislike this alternative would like parents to believe that home schooled children will be socially stagnated or social misfits. In fact, some educators believe that parents who choose this type of education must be social misfits themselves. For some reason, the very act of choosing to educate their own children sets parents up as radicals, when in fact they are choosing to do it for very logical and rational reasons.

Sometimes friends, neighbors, and relatives are also critical about a family's decision to home school. They may be afraid that the children will not learn how to get along with other children. Their comments range from 'Jonathan will become too dependent on his parents' to 'Maureen will be left out of all the fun.'

These critics all seem to believe that the only way for children to learn social skills is at school, and that the family environment is lacking in this fundamental area.

'I don't agree with educators on that aspect,' said one home schooler. And evidence from parents, child psychologists, and even from the children themselves all substantiates claims from home schoolers that their children are not becoming socially inept. Quite the contrary. Evidence points to the opposite. Children educated at home seem to have far greater social confidence than their public schooled peers."

Gorder concludes her discussion of socialization with this passionate statement (capitals in the original):

A government study reports that hundreds of thousands of secondary school students are physically attacked EACH MONTH, and that several million have something stolen in that same month. The same study found that one in four elementary students are afraid that somebody [another student] might hurt them at school.

THIS IS THE TYPE OF SOCIALIZATION THAT EDUCATORS ARE WORRIED ABOUT HOME SCHOOLERS MISSING?"[13]

Mario Pagnoni, in *The Complete Home Educator: A Comprehensive Guide to Modern Home-teaching* (1984), was quite eloquent in this discussion of the socialization issue, noting that

> "The issue of socialization is THE BIG ONE for critics of school-at-home. Indeed, it is almost the first concern people raise when they meet unschoolers. Many think that, no matter what intellectual and emotional gains are made, school-at-home is doomed to failure, because *of the lack of peer contacts.* Home-school critics quite generally agree that schools are not very social places. They know that schoolchildren are discouraged from talking with each other, sometimes even while passing in the halls or during lunch. They are aware that children are sometimes segregated from the 'opposite sex' for classes and at lunch and recess time. It comes as no revelation to them that the peer group likes to find a scapegoat on which to vent its collective anger, frustration, and cruelty. Yes, all of this is eminently clear to them. Nonetheless, these critics still favor the conventional system. Their argument goes like this: 'That is the way the world is. The sooner kids learn to fit into the system, the better. If you shelter your children from THE REAL WORLD, they will never learn to deal with it.'
>
> It seems to me that a parent's job is to provide as much as possible for his children that is positive, and to remove as much as possible that is negative. Many parents have reasoned that, since school was having a negative impact on their child, and home-education was a viable alternative for them, home-schooling was not only their right, but their duty as a parent.

People have this false notion that children educated at home are vacuum packed in some hermetically sealed environment. Home-schoolers move around in the real world every day. They interact with adults as well as with children. They enjoy daytime access to the community. Their school friends come home in mid-afternoon. Besides, the 'real world' argument sounds too much like, 'I love my child, so I fill his life with negative things to prepare him for the tough life ahead.'

I'm not interested in raising children who passively submit to all that is negative in the 'real world.' I want children who can see clearly that the system is imperfect -- children who are skeptical enough to know that those in authority are not *always* to be trusted, but not cynical to the point that they trust no one. …. I want children who can think for themselves, who refuse to be swallowed up by what has been called 'groupthink' – the kind of collective decision-making preferred by so many of our young people. Perhaps, in some small way, these 'different' children can help improve the system. That system changes extremely slowly, to be sure. But we are all part of it. As we change, the system changes."[14]

In their edited book, *Schooling at Home: Parents, Kids, and Learning*, Anne Pedersen and Peggy O'Mara covered the socialization question quite thoroughly. In the book's preface, Peggy O'Mara honestly and openly shared her personal concerns on the matter:

"Although I felt strongly that the kind of socialization characteristic of the early years in school is often more harmful to children than helpful, I sometimes wondered if my children were meeting 'enough' friends."[15]

Later in this same book, when the issue of socialization is raised, the following admission is made:

"We are forced unexpectedly to concede . . . that not only are children better taught at home than at school during their first 10 or 12 years but they are also far better socialized. Stanford's Albert Bandura observes that the tendency toward dependency on peers rather than family for basic values has in recent years moved down to preschools. Contrary to popular belief, children normally are best socialized by parents, not other kids; in fact, adds Bronfenbrenner, the more children in a group, the fewer meaningful human contacts they have.

We found that socialization is not neutral. It is either positive or negative. Positive, or altruistic and principled, sociability is firmly linked with the family in both quantity and quality of self-confidence, self-respect, and self-worth. This is, in turn, dependent largely on the values and experiences provided by the family at least until the child can reason consistently. In other words, the child who works, eats, plays, has his rest, and is read to daily more with his parents than with his peers senses that he or she is a part of the family corporation – and, as such, is needed, wanted, and depended upon. Such a child is more often a thinker than a mere repeater of other children's thoughts. He or she is independent and self-directed in values and skills, and largely avoids peer dependency."[16]

Susan and Michael Card (the well-known Christian musician/composer, and his wife) authored their own book on home schooling, entitled *The Homeschool Journey*. When addressing the issue of socialization, they begin by describing a friend's humorous response to the infamous question:

"One of my friends would answer this question by saying, 'We try to avoid it!' Her response is humorous to those of us close to her because, though we realize the importance of 'good' socialization, we think the term is getting an inordinate amount of attention. Why isn't there as much emphasis on learning to be self-governing and on individuality?

The best way to deal with socialization is to clearly define it. According to Webster's definition, *socialize* first means 'to make social; adjust to or make fit for cooperative group living.' I believe we are doing a very good job of this in our own home. We are educating and equipping our children with a moral base, sound judgment, discernment, and plenty of occasions for interaction both at home and with friends and family.

The second definition is 'to adapt or make conform to the common needs of a social group.' First we must answer the question, What social group are we conforming to? And how much time do we want to commit to social groups? If we send our children to school, they get 30 to 40 hours a week of social group time. Then there are extracurricular group activities that occur after school. Could this perhaps be too much of a good thing? How do homeschoolers implement this aspect of socialization? Our involvement with our churches is a great example. Other social groups would include our families, friends, our organized homeschool groups and outings, co-op classes, Boy Scouts or Girl Scouts, or outside classes like ballet, gymnastics, or organized sports. These are all examples of wholesome social groups that are usually well supervised.

And is socialization always good in itself? There is good, positive socialization, and there is bad socialization. To achieve good socialization in young children there must be close supervision. The ratio between students and teachers is too great in the public school system to achieve this effectively. I have seen 'good socialization' take place when Nathan is in his group session, with as little as four children to one teacher and an aide. Every altercation is addressed, and an appropriate response is given and practiced . . . .

The last definition of *socialization* is 'to subject to governmental ownership and control; nationalize.' No thank you. We have lost too many lives for the sake of freedom of individuality to make ourselves slaves to government protocol. If our government officials would look and listen, they would see rising a great movement that will produce some of the best citizens this country has seen in a long while."[17]

Michael Farris -- founder and former president of the Home School Legal Defense Association, and founder and current president of the first home schooling-centered institute of higher learning, Patrick Henry College -- understandably had a lot to say about the socialization issue in *The Future of Home Schooling: A New Direction for Christian Home Education.* As Farris noted,

"Anyone who has been home schooling longer than two weeks has been asked this question dozens of times. It was the first question I asked when I first heard of home schooling in 1982.

First of all, it is fair to say that home schooling does not eliminate socialization, but it does separate socialization and academics to a considerable degree. If one gives even five seconds of thought to that, it should be immediately recognized that this is a plus and not a minus for home schooling. ....

Much of what goes on in public schools is an inappropriate mix of socialization and academics. Children whisper, slip notes to each other, gaze longingly at their latest flame, or do any number of socially oriented activities while the teacher is trying his or her best to impart some material. And so it goes without saying that much of the socialization that is common these days is plainly wrong in any setting. Drugs, alcohol, and premarital sex are all part of the socialization scene that home schoolers miss out on during their academic day (and to a great extent they miss out on these things altogether). ....

On a more technical level, socialization is properly understood by professional sociologists as the method by which we teach the next generation the rules of society. Do we really want six-year-olds responsible for socializing each other? Isn't it better for our children to learn the rules of society and the values that make society work from responsible adults? But the fact is that children get their socialization values from whomever they spend a majority of their time [sic]. If they spend a majority of their time with other six-year-olds, they get their fundamental values from their peers. If they spend a majority of time with their parents and family, then parents are the source of that child's fundamental values. If you doubt this, project ahead until age fourteen or so. How many fourteen-year-olds are more influenced by their peers than their parents? I rest my case. ....

The kind of socialization that results from peer-dependent institutional schools is contrary to the way all the rest of life works. Where else in society do people go around in packs of age-segregated herds?"[18]

Another well-known and highly regarded home schooling book was authored by the Colfaxes. In 1988, David and Micki Colfax wrote *Homeschooling for Excellence*, and addressed the issue of socialization in the chapter entitled, "Some Homeschooling Questions and Answers":

"Q. What about the socialization of homeschooled children? Aren't they too isolated from their peers?

A. In the first place, homeschooled children are seldom, if ever, socially isolated. Indeed, precisely because they have more opportunities to interact with a wide range of people, they tend to become socially competent and socially responsible at an earlier age than most of their conventionally schooled peers. The argument that socialization is the *primary* function of the schools--and educators are increasingly claiming just that as their failure to develop the intellect becomes more and more obvious--ignores evidence that peer group pressure in the schools, except in some very special contexts, does little to foster intellectual growth or the acquisition of desirable social values."[19]

Ray E. Ballmann, in *The How and Why of Home Schooling*, included a similar chapter, entitled "Common Questions About Home Schooling." Ballmann answered the asked question in a highly succinct and logical manner, as follows:

"Will my child miss out on socialization?

This is a common misconception. Popular opinion assumes that children need to extensively be around others their own age to be properly socialized. This dangerous assumption leads well-intentioned parents to false conclusions. So powerful is this psychological notion that many parents concede to the viability of academic instruction at home but keep their children in the public educational setting in order to help them develop and master their social skills. Sound research, however, lends little credibility to this socialization theory.

There are two types of socialization, positive and negative. Positive sociability builds responsibility, cooperation, kindness, fidelity, love, and bilateral trust. Negative sociability is the result of coerced age-segregation and builds rivalry, contention, selfishness, peer-dependency, criticism, and derision. It molds a poor self-esteem that responds quickly to peer pressure.

Without a doubt, a loving, outreaching home environment is the best socializer a young child could possibly have. A home-schooled child tends to mix freely with all ages and not just a narrow age grouping. Home schoolers on average score higher than their conventionally-schooled peers in tests that measure both self-concept and sociability. A young child learns good sociability primarily by watching and mirroring. Do you want your child to model after you or after his peers, after his teachers at school or his teachers at home? What kind of socialization do you want for your child, positive or negative? The evidence is overwhelming that shows where each kind is bred and nurtured."[20]

Dr. Raymond and Dorothy Moore -- two well-known and highly respected home school advocates -- explore the socialization issue in *The Successful Homeschool Family Handbook: A Creative and Stress-Free Approach to Homeschooling*. Indeed, they have an entire chapter devoted to it, entitled "How Can They Possibly Be Socialized?" This in-depth chapter (a) deals with issues of peer dependence and self-concept, (b) discusses briefly some relevant research, and (c) offers some common sense solutions.

In the beginning of this chapter, the Moores also offer some interesting and thought-provoking background to the entire discussion, which certainly bears repeating:

"In recent years, since most alert educators have found that children taught some or entirely in the home average much higher in achievement, they have been compelled to find another bone to pick. It was quite a task, but most of the critics finally settled on *socialization*. And they have been busy picking the old bone blanched and white. Yet if they are honest and still reading and listening, they eventually discover, usually to their surprise, that the socialization picture in the home is even more dramatic and consistently encouraging than achievement. And the evidence from both research and history is powerful and . . . understandable."[21]

In *The Ultimate Guide to Homeschooling*, Debra Bell answers frequently asked questions about home schooling, including her designated question #5:

"But What About Socialization?

Of course this section wouldn't be complete without addressing the number-one FAQ posed to homeschoolers. Some folks seem to expect our kids to be as clueless in social situations as the *Beverly Hillbillies*. But if you spend even a little bit of time among homeschoolers you'll realize this is a nonissue.

First, let's define our terms. Make a list of what you mean by *socialization.* Here's mine:
* Kid can work cooperatively with other people, including those from different backgrounds and beliefs.
* Kid is not socially awkward in group situation.
* Kid can work out differences with others.
* Kid understands appropriate behavior in social situations.

Now let me ask you this: Where did you learn appropriate social behavior? School? Where did you learn to appreciate folks who dress differently, act differently, think differently? School? Where did you learn proper etiquette? High school cafeteria? Get the point?

Homeschooled kids can learn in a much broader context of social experiences than they would in school. Typically it is an age-integrated environment. They are frequently in group settings with adults, senior citizens, toddlers, and peers. There is none of this silliness about sixth graders not talking to fifth graders or big brothers not talking to younger sisters. There is no pecking order to fall in line with or acceptance measured by the clothes you wear or the dares you take."[22]

Some useful thoughts about this issue can also be found on the *Home Education Magazine* website. In their question and answer section, they respond to the following concern: "How will my child learn to get along in the world?"

> "A. This is the question homeschoolers often grimace about and call the "S" question (socialization). The real concern, it seems, is whether homeschooled children will be able to function out in the world if they don't have the experiences schooled children have.
>
> Think for a moment about what schools really do. They classify and segregate children by age and ability, reinforce class, gender and racial prejudice, and strip from children the right to any real interaction or private life. Socialization, in this respect, becomes submitting one's will to that of the group (or person in charge). This is not the basis for healthy relationships. Home educated children, because they spend so much of their time out in the real world, generally are able to communicate well with both adults and children and to have friends of all ages. They choose to spend time with others because they enjoy their company or have a similar interest -- just like adults."[23]

Cindy Short offers a valuable Christian viewpoint on social development in *The Teaching Home* (2000, Summer):

> "As we go about the day-to-day work of educating and training our children, it is important that we keep in mind our ultimate purpose as Christians -- to be lights in a dark world, pointing the lost to our Savior, the Light of the World.

A related purpose that we share as Christians is to encourage and build one another up for our individual and corporate ministries. These purposes can only be accomplished as we and our children relate effectively and spiritually to those around us. Thus the area of social development is also foundational.

In considering how best to provide for our children's social development, we may be faced with a bewildering array of conflicting ideas and opportunities. But we are not without guidance.

We must evaluate each decision in the light of our ultimate purposes and the written Word of God. We also have the spiritual and practical insights of other Christian home educators. .... May our children's social development prepare them to 'shine as lights in the world' (Philippians 2:15 KJV)."[24]

Later on, in this same issue of *The Teaching Home*, Cindy Short teams with Sue Welch to expound further on the issue in an article aptly and simply titled, "What About Socialization?":

"Many anxious grandparents, neighbors, and even parents wonder, Can a child develop adequately when he is home schooled?

This is a legitimate concern. However, the assumption that children are adequately socialized at school is unfortunately false. The reality of today's school-produced socialization is seen lived out in the negative behavior of many children and young people in the neighborhood, at the shopping mall, or in tragic newspaper headlines.

The feared outcomes of teaching children at home (e.g., inability to relate to or work with others, insecurity, antisocial behavior) have been found to be unsubstantiated. ....

The presumption that children must attend school to be part of 'the real world' breaks down when you consider that nowhere in adult life is there a situation like the one that exists in an age-segregated classroom. The daily life of a family in their home and community is far more real than any school can even simulate (although some try to do just that).

Some critics of home education charge that parents are overprotective, sheltering their children in the 'hothouse environment' of their own homes.

However, any gardener who has attempted to grow delicate plants in a harsh climate knows that it would be foolish to start those plants outdoors. They must be protected and sheltered from extremes of cold or heat and from animals, insects, fungus, or disease that would attack them.

Only when these plants have an established root system, strong stems, and plenty of leaves will they be gradually exposed to the outside environment and eventually transplanted.

It is a loving act of kindness to guard and care for your children in this nurturing manner in their childhood and youth.

Fears that home-schooled children will never 'fit in' to a group or that they will not learn to handle temptation are also unsubstantiated. Again, school children are more likely to suffer these outcomes from the less-than-ideal group dynamics present in even a Christian or other private school. ....

The truth is that effective, positive socialization requires more attention from caring adults than is available in an institutionalized setting. Thus, home educators are privileged with superior opportunities to socialize their children. Far from being a drawback of home schooling, socialization is one of its strongest advantages.

Within a family, love and acceptance of your child can give him needed security, even when he is being corrected and disciplined. In this setting he can be properly 'socialized' through training in both character qualities and social skills. It remains for concerned parents (whether home schooling or not) to define specific goals and choose effective methods for their children's socialization."[25]

Hearing From: Home Schooled Children

In *A Sense of Self: Listening to Homeschooled Adolescent Girls* (1995), by S. Sheffer, we find a young homeschooled woman who has an interesting "take" on the advantages of home school socialization. Sheffer relates that

"Meredith, applying to college a year after I interviewed her, wrote in one of her application essays that . . .

'My outlook on life has been affected in many, many ways by homeschooling. .... I have grown up in an atmosphere of tolerance for individuality. Kids in school can have a hard time discovering who they are, in part because they have only other kids to compare themselves to. If all the other kids are the same (externally), it can be scary to be seen as different in any way.

I have had the chance to become a strong individual and to know who I am, if not who I will be. In the past three years I have been living in what I would call 'real life,' interacting with people in many different situations and coming to a thorough understanding of myself and why I do what I do.'"[26]

Amanda Bergson-Shilcock is a homeschooled girl who wrote her own pamphlet to give out concerning the issue of socialization. She had the following pronouncement to make (capitals in the original):

"THE MOST WIDELY HELD HOMESCHOOLING MISCONCEPTION OF ALL TIME:
    That homeschoolers will never become 'socialized.' I would say that one hundred out of every hundred people who ever found out I was homeschooling asked me this question in one form or another. This is what I usually say to them:

'Well, you know, a lot of people ask that question. I actually think homeschooling offers better options in some cases than schools. For instance, in a school setting, one is likely to find many people of one's *own* age range (say, within two to three years), but with middle schools and high schools in separate buildings most of the time you never even see people significantly older or younger than you. I count myself very lucky to have, in addition to friends my own age, many close adult friends, and a good number of younger friends.'"[27]

Yet another homeschooled teenager, Rebecca Merrion, offers her own viewpoint:

"I don't think that homeschooled teenagers get into the commercialism of the world nearly as much as teenagers who to go school. For some reason, everyone in school wears and does the same thing that everyone else does, be it *Guess* jeans, punk hair, or continually hanging out at the mall. I am glad that some homeschoolers feel they can be anyone that they want to be, unlike most of the kids that go to school and feel that they all have to be alike, or else they don't fit in and are called weird. Not only individual spirit and taste are lost in school, but responsibility also, because in school kids hardly ever have to do anything for themselves except spit back memorized information. And yet they put up with it for thirteen years – not including college."[28]

Conclusions

In this chapter, we have heard from home schooling parents, home schooled children, and a variety of home schooling experts about the issue of socialization. What conclusions may we safely draw from their observations? Clearly, at this point, most home schoolers are rather irritated by the question and what it implies, and see socialization as a significant "plus" factor in home schooling rather than a negative. Their own experiences with home schooling have borne this belief out.

"Ah," the unpersuaded reader may say, "but all these are people closely aligned and allied, in one manner or another, with the home schooling movement -- of course their 'take' on the issue is going to be a positive one!"

This last point actually does have some merit, which is why the following chapter presents a detailed and thorough examination of the current research on socialization in home schooling. In other words, whereas this chapter informed us as to the beliefs of home schoolers, the next chapter will inform us as to the results of educational and psychological research studies which investigated this issue.

Endnotes – Chapter II

[1] (p. 11). Griffith, M. (1997). *The homeschooling handbook.* Rocklin, CA: Prima.

[2] (p. 223). Meehan, G. (1993). A parent's perspective. In G. Llewellyn (Ed.), *Real lives: Eleven teenagers who don't go to school* (pp. 222-224). Eugene, OR: Lowry House.

[3] Available online at:
http://members.mint.net/caronfam/Faqs.html (retrieved 7/17/01).

[4] (pp. xxi-xxii). Griffith, M. (1997). *The homeschooling handbook.* Rocklin, CA: Prima.

[5] (p. 11). Griffith, M. (1997). *The homeschooling handbook.* Rocklin, CA: Prima.

[6] (p. 12). Griffith, M. (1997). *The homeschooling handbook.* Rocklin, CA: Prima.

[7] (p. 12). Griffith, M. (1997). *The homeschooling handbook.* Rocklin, CA: Prima.

[8] Available online at: http://www.madrone.com/Home-ed/hs2.htm (retrieved 7/3/2001).

[9] (pp. 44-45). Holt, J. (1981). *Teach your own: A hopeful path for education.* New York: Delacorte Press/Seymour Lawrence.

[10] (pp. 2-3). Mayberry, M., Knowles, J. G., Ray, B. D., & Marlow, S. (1995). *Home schooling: Parents as educators.* Thousand Oaks, CA: Corwin Press.

[11] (p. 119). Medlin, R. G. (2000). Home schooling and the question of socialization. *Peabody Journal of Education, 75* (1 & 2), 107-123.

[12] (pp. 51-53). Guterson, D. (1992). *Family matters: Why homeschooling makes sense.* New York: Harcourt Brace.

[13] (pp. 43-45, 47). Gorder, C. (1985). *Home schools: An alternative.* Columbus, OH: Blue Bird.

[14] (pp. 191-193). Pagnoni, M. (1984). *The complete home educator: A comprehensive guide to modern home-teaching.* New York: Larson.

[15] (p. ix). Pedersen, A., & O'Mara, P. (Eds.). (1990). *Schooling at home: Parents, kids, and learning.* Santa Fe, NM: John Muir Publications/Mothering Magazine.

[16] (p. 26). Pedersen, A., & O'Mara, P. (Eds.). (1990). *Schooling at home: Parents, kids, and learning.* Santa Fe, NM: John Muir Publications/Mothering Magazine.

[17] (pp. 177-179). Card, S., & Card, M. (1997). *The homeschool journey.* Eugene, OR: Harvest House.

[18] (pp. 123-124). Farris, M. (1997). *The future of home schooling: A new direction for Christian home education.* Washington, DC: Regnery.

[19] (pp. 101-102). Colfax, D., & Colfax, M. (1988). *Homeschooling for excellence.* New York: Warner Books.

[20] (pp. 185-186). Ballmann, R.E. (1995). *The how and why of home schooling* (2nd ed.). Wheaton, IL: Crossway Books.

[21] (p. 48). Moore, R., & Moore, D. (1994). *The successful homeschool family handbook: A creative and stress-free approach to homeschooling.* Nashville, TN: Thomas Nelson.

[22] (pp. 48-49). Bell, D. (1997). *The ultimate guide to homeschooling.* Nashville, TN: Thomas Nelson.

[23] From the Home Education Magazine website: http://www.home-ed-magazine.com/INF/STRT/STRT_faq.html

[24] Short, C. (2000, Summer). Character training and social development. *The Teaching Home,* p. 39.

[25] (p. 47). Welch, S., & Short, C. (2000, Summer). What About Socialization? *The Teaching Home,* pp. 44-51.

26 (pp. 180-181). Sheffer, S. (1995). *A sense of self: Listening to homeschooled adolescent girls.* Portsmouth, NH: Heinemann.

27 (p. 272). Bergson-Shilcock, A. (1993). Homeschooling is another word for "living." In G. Llewellyn (Ed.), *Real lives: Eleven teenagers who don't go to school* (pp. 268-293). Eugene, OR: Lowry House.

28 (p. 91). Merrion, R. (1993). Giving my time. In G. Llewellyn (Ed.), *Real lives: Eleven teenagers who don't go to school* (pp. 88-105) Eugene, OR: Lowry House.

Chapter III

What Does the Research Have to Say?

W hat did the educational researchers who investigated the issue of home schooling and socialization find? This chapter is dedicated to answering this question in great detail. The research studies will be presented in chronological order (and alphabetically by researcher within those years in which more than one study occurred), with the actual abstract of the study provided where possible. Abstracts can be particularly helpful when assessing a study, because they normally include a very brief summation of the guiding research question(s) of the study, the methodology employed, and the final results. Various commentaries on the research are also included.

In an effort to be as absolutely thorough and comprehensive as possible in presenting research dealing with socialization and home schooling, a great many studies are included whose primary focus was not necessarily solely or specifically the issue of socialization, but which nevertheless included findings having to do with some aspect of socialization.

Following, then, is a look at 24 pertinent home schooling research studies, spanning the years from 1985 to the present.

1985 Research Study: Schemmer

Title: "Case Studies of Four Families Engaged in Home Education"

Author: Dr. Beverly Ann S. Schemmer

Abstact of the Study

"The purpose of the study was to give a description of the curricula and methods used in the home schools of home educator and to evaluate by means of case studies the effects of home education upon those included in the study. Chapter 1 presented an overview of the background and significance for the study and five research questions which were addressed by the study. The questions were: (1) Will students being educated in the home be able to obtain academic achievement at comparable levels with those students being educated in the public school? (2) Will students being educated in the home be able to show at least one year's gain in academic achievement when scores of the previous year are compared with scores from the current year? (3) What curricula and methods are being used in the home education of the children involved in the study? (4) What attitudes and values motivated the parents in the study to home educate their children? (5) What legal actions, if any, did the parents included in the study face as a result of their choice to home educate? Chapter II provided a review of related literature. Reviewed were: compulsory attendance laws, related court decisions, and research related to home education. Chapter III presented the plan of organization and procedures used in gathering, reporting, and summarizing the data. Chapter IV contained the data collected from the four home educators. The data were presented in narrative form and in tables for each family case study. Chapter V presented a summary of the case studies, answers to research questions, observations, and recommendations. The data provided the following answers to the five research questions: (1) Forty percent of the home educated students scored equal to the median national score. (2) Students showed inconsistencies in average gains for the year. (3) Three of the four families used curriculum materials commercially prepared for home educators. (4) *The parent educators appeared motivated by socialization concerns and desires for values training* [emphasis added]. (5) Legal action was taken against one of the four families in the study."[1]

Only one of the five research questions utilized by Dr. Schemmer had any bearing on or relationship to the issue of socialization, and it is the data gathered in response to this research question that is of particular interest to us here. Specifically, what response was received to the fourth research question—"What attitudes and values motivated the parents in the study to home educate their children?"

According to Schemmer (cited in Ray, 1987), "Those attitudes and values which appeared to be most meaningful regarding their reasons for home educating were related to the areas of socialization and value training desires of the parents .... "[2] According to Dr. Brian Ray in his review of this research study, "Schemmer also offered some general observations about the four families." The two most pertinent to the issue of socialization include the following:

> "All of the children in the study were readily able to communicate with the researcher and made her feel that they were glad to be a part of the study," and "All of the children in the study were engaged in other groups outside the home which offered opportunities for social contacts with other children."[3]

Clearly, the results of this study indicate that (a) socialization was an important part of the parents' decision to home school, (b) the children involved in the study were able to communicate effectively with the researcher, and (c) the children involved in the study were also involved in socialization opportunities with others outside the family.

1986 Research Studies: Delahooke & Taylor

Delahooke

Title: "Home Educated Children's Social/Emotional Adjustment and Academic Achievement: A Comparative Study"

Author: Dr. Mona Maarse Delahooke

Abstract of the Study

"The purpose of this exploratory study was to ascertain if any differences exist between traditionally educated children and children educated at home in the areas of social/emotional adjustment and academic achievement. The study utilized a non-experimental design which included one comparison group. Sixty children between the ages of 7 and 12 were recruited from two private schools, a home education organization, and through networking of participating subjects. The home educated group was comprised of 28 children, with an average age of 9.2 years. The comparison group consisted of 32 children with an average age of 9.0 years. Each child was individually tested at his/her home by either the primary researcher or a research assistant.

During the testing session, the subject's parent filled out a brief demographic questionnaire. The following instruments were administered to each child: the Reading and Arithmetic sections of the Wide Range Achievement Test-Revised (Jastak & Wilkinson, 1984), the Block Design and Vocabulary subtests of the Wechsler Intelligence Scale for Children-Revised (Wechsler, 1974), the Roberts Apperception Test for Children (McArthur & Roberts, 1982), and a brief sentence completion task.

An analysis of covariance was conducted to determine if the groups would differ in the area of achievement, while controlling for the effects of intelligence. Univariate t-tests for independent samples were conducted to determine if any differences would exist between the groups on the RATC. The statistical analysis revealed no significant differences between the two groups on academic achievement levels or measured intelligence. Additionally, both groups scored in the well-adjusted range of the RATC.

However, significant differences were evident in the area of social relationships. The home educated children appeared to be less peer-oriented than the comparison group. Subjects educated in the private schools exhibited a significantly greater focus on peers and non-family individuals than did the home educated group. The results of the study suggest that the home educated children's achievement functioning is similar to that of children educated in a private school, while differences appear to exist in the area of perceived peer influence [emphasis added]."[4]

Delahooke's study was an important first step in directly addressing, through research, the ever-present question regarding socialization in home schooling. The results of her research are cited quite frequently, as in the following from the web site of the *National Home Education Research Institute*: "[According to Delahooke's research], the home schooled are well adjusted socially and emotionally like their private school comparison group. The home educated, however, are less peer dependent than the private school students."[5]

Delahooke's research findings naturally found their way into an article on the socialization question in a home schooling magazine:

"Dr. Mona Delahooke studied the social and emotional development of 9 – year - olds from private schools compared to those who were home schooled. The only significant difference was that 'private school subjects appeared to be more influenced by or concerned with peers than the home-educated group.' It appeared that home-educated children perceived their parents as primary authority figures more often than did the private school children."[6]

While Delahooke's research study was quite important and noteworthy in that it was the first to look at the socialization issue, her study also investigated the academic achievement of home schooled children vs. privately schooled children. The very first study to specifically examine *only* the issue of socialization was conducted by John Wesley Taylor; it is detailed in the following section.

Taylor

Title: "Self-Concept in Home-Schooling Children"

Author: Dr. John Wesley Taylor, V

Abstract of the Study

"The home school appears to be in a renaissance. This national study sought to provide an empirical base upon which to formulate viable decisions regarding home-schooling children. The study considered homeschoolers in grades four through twelve. The randomized sample yielded 224 qualified participants.

Conclusions include the following: (1) The self-concept of the homeschoolers was significantly higher (p < .001) than that of the conventionally schooled population on all scales of the Piers-Harris Children's Self-Concept Scale. Half of the home-schoolers scored at or above the 91st percentile on the global scale. (2) Insofar as self-concept is a reflector of socialization, it appears that few homeschoolers are socially deprived. (3) The self-concept of the homeschoolers decreases significantly (p < .01) as age and grade level rise. (4) The factors of gender, gender [sic], number of siblings, locale of residence, prior conventional schooling, number of years of home schooling, beginning school age, educational level of home-school operators, and geographical region are not significantly related to the self-concept of homeschoolers when considered independently. (5) Higher socioeconomic status and an increase in the number of homeschoolers in a family are significantly related (p < .05) to a more positive self-concept in homeschoolers.

(6) The best predictive model of self-concept in homeschoolers (p < .001) is related to lower grade-equivalence, higher years of home schooling, higher socioeconomic status, higher number of homeschoolers in the family, and higher beginning school age. The model is statistically stable and accounts for over 12 percent of the variance in the self-concept. (7) Homeschoolers are apparently concentrated towards lower grade levels and tend to commence formal instruction at a later age than the national average. (8) There is an approximately balanced distribution of homeschoolers in terms of gender and geographical region. (9) It appears that home-schooling families frequently have more children that the national average and usually have more than a single child in the home school. (10) Very few of the children are in their first year of home schooling and most have previously attended a conventional school. (11) The educational level and socio-economic status attained by home-school operators seems to be considerably higher and their locale more rural than that of the comparable general population."[7]

As with Delahooke's important study, Taylor's groundbreaking research is cited frequently, as in the very brief summation found on the *NHERI's* web page: "Dr. Taylor (1986) found that the home educated have significantly higher self concepts than those in public schools."[8]

A more detailed description of Taylor's research, albeit still necessarily brief, was given by Dr. Brian Ray of the NHERI in an article on socialization for a home schooling magazine:

> "Dr. John Wesley Taylor focused on self-concept as one significant aspect of the psychological development of children. His nationwide study revealed that the self-concept of home-school students was significantly higher than that of public school students for the global scale and all six subscales of the Piers-Harris Children's Self-Concept Scale (PHCSCS)."[9]

1987 Research Study: Wartes

Title: "Washington Homeschool Research Project Report from the 1986 Homeschool Testing and Other Descriptive Information About Washington's Homeschoolers"

Author: Jon Wartes

Jon Wartes, according to the *Home Centered Learning Annotated Bibliography* (11th ed.), "has been a public school teacher and counselor for 21 years," and is "presently head counselor at a large suburban area high school; and a home schooling parent." [10]

While there is no abstract as such for this particular research article, a summary article based on the 1986 study noted above should provide all relevant data. In this article, Wartes describes the purpose of his research project, as well as the population and sample utilized. The purpose was "to provide (a) base line information about the achievement levels of Washington home schoolers and (b) descriptive information about those who choose this educational option"; the population and sample were made up of "Washington home schoolers who are apparently in conformance with the home school law constituted the population. .... All descriptive information . . . was obtained through a 112-item questionnaire that was distributed via 12 'local coordinators' (support group leaders, test service operators, and others) throughout the state. A total of 219 questionnaires were returned."[11]

Now that we are familiar with the details of how this study was conducted and with whom, let's look at the single question Wartes asked in this research study that is of particular interest to us here, that question being, "Are Home Schooled Children Being Socially Isolated?" Wartes answers this question with the following:

> "Based upon these data [from the questionnaires], the answer is no. Respondents indicated a median of 20 to 29 hours per month for (a) participation in organized community activities, (b) contact with age peers, and (c) contact with non-age peers outside the immediate family. Parents rated 94% or more of their children as average or above in skills such as (a) ability to constructively interact with peers, (b) ability to constructively interact with adults, (c) [ability to] display leadership ability, and (d) [ability to] to show a sense of responsibility."[12]

1989 Research Study: Montgomery

Title: "The Effect of Home Schooling on the Leadership Skills of Home Schooled Students"

Author: Dr. Linda Ruth Montgomery

Abstract of the Study

"The dissertation examines the growing home schooling movement and addresses the question, 'What is the effect of home schooling on the leadership skills of home schooled students?' Chapter 1 provides a background of the study, particularly of the leadership issue. Chapter 2 reviews the literature on the statistics, motivations, and characteristics of this country's home schoolers. Chapter 3 reviews the literature on the historical roots and the legal issues surrounding home schooling, particularly the compulsory school attendance laws.

Chapter 4 reviews the literature on leadership and what the research says are the predictors in childhood and adolescence of adult leadership. Because most of the literature focuses on adolescents and preadolescents, only students age ten and older were included in this study.

Chapter 5 describes the study. Parents and students in fifty home schooling families in Washington State were interviewed in the summer and fall of 1988. Interview questions were designed to elicit data related particularly to those variables the literature suggests are links to leadership: (1) family conditions and environment, and (2) student participation in extracurricular activities. A random sample of same age and sex students in a conventional school were also interviewed to provide a point of comparison with the home schooling students.

Chapter 6 and 7 display and analyze the data. Chapter 6 focuses on the secondary data, which are related to the motivations and practices of Washington's home schoolers.

Chapter 7 focuses on the primary data, the extracurricular program of the home school and parent expectations regarding independent and leadership behaviors in their children. The participation rates of home schooling students in activities such as sports, community service, church youth groups, and jobs are compared with those of the conventionally schooled students. It is concluded that fewer significant differences exist between the two groups than would be expected.

Chapter 8 summarizes the findings and makes recommendations for secondary school educators, home schooling parents, and researchers interested in this topic."[13]

In sum, according to the NHERI website, "Dr. Montgomery (1989) found that home schooled students are just as involved in out-of-school and extracurricular activities that predict leadership in adulthood as are those in the comparison private school (that was comprised of students more involved than those in public schools)."[14]

More particularly, Montgomery concluded from the results of her study that "it would appear that home schooling is not generally repressive of a student's potential leadership, and may in fact, nurture leadership at least as well as does the conventional system."[15]

And most importantly to the specific purpose of this book, Montgomery also concluded, as a result of her study, that

"home schooled adolescents are not isolated from social interaction with their peer group nor denied participation in a variety of at-home and out-of-home organized group activities.... The perception of home schooled students as being isolated, uninvolved, and protected from peer contact is simply not supported by this data. To the contrary, there were a number of students who reported having increased social contact and group participation because school required less of their time [emphasis added]."[16]

1990 Research Study: Beaven

Title: "Living and Learning: A Phenomenological Study of Home Education"

Author: Dr. Claudia Carolynne Beaven

Abstract of the Study

"Home education from the parents [sic] perspective is described through a phenomenological study. Twenty-nine families were interviewed (recorded using audio tapes) and observed (descriptive notes were written), over a period of live [sic] years. Four of these families are presented by way of portraits. Each portrait is personal to the family of focus, however each in their own way covers the major themes arising from the analysis. A composite picture emerges providing an understanding of these parent/educators [sic] experiences. The themes discussed are: The family – the focal point of the lived-world; The parents views of, and concerns about, the socialization of the children; Perspectives on time, how it is viewed and used; and The parents – independent thinkers in search of freedom. The message from the informants is that living and learning can not be separated, as they feel the schools attempt to do. They see learning to be based in life experience; occurring as the child is ready and in the direction of his interests. This I have called 'Connected Learning.' Connected learning requires a warm, nurturing environment where the parent trusts the child will learn. When connected learning is experienced over a period of several years the child lives in 'balance' between the internal world of the self, and the external world of knowledge. Key elements of connected learning are the home, time, trust, freedom, and community. The apparent success of home education suggests that in order to help children learn how to learn: they need to have living and learning integrated; they need to feel secure; they need to be with teachers who truly care about them; they need to be with teachers who can 'get-out-of-the-way' of the child's learning; they need to spend less time on pre-planned curriculums and more time in pursuit of their own interests; they need to be trusted to learn; and *they need time to interact within the communities in which they live and less time in large same-age peer groups* [emphasis added]. Suggestions are made for further research in the area of home education and training.[17]

According to the participants in Beaven's study, home schooling families believe that their children "need time to interact within the communities in which they live," while spending "less time in same-age peer groups." Although "socialization" as a term is not used here, the issues being dealt with are clearly the same.

1990 Research Study: Knowles

According to the NHERI website,

"Dr. Gary Knowles, of the University of Michigan, explored adults who were home educated. None were unemployed and none were on welfare, 94% said home education prepared them to be independent persons, 79% said it helped them interact with individuals from different levels of society, and they strongly supported the home education method."[18]

Dr. Knowles's research was of such interest to the home schooling community that Michael Farris (founder and former president of the Home School Defense Association) made it a specific topic of discussion on a radio program. Following is a transcript of that broadcast.

(Announcer) "Will home schooled graduates be equipped with the skills they need to function in society? Join us on Home School Heartbeat as Michael Farris, president of the Home School Legal Defense Association, shares the results of some interesting research on home educated adults.

(Michael Farris) A recent study by Dr. Gary Knowles, Assistant Professor of Education at the University of Michigan, confirms what home schooling parents have known for years. Teaching children at home won't make them social misfits. Listen to what he discovered. First, none of the home educated adults he surveyed was unemployed or on welfare. Second, more than three-quarters felt that being taught at home actually helped them to interact with people from different levels of society. Third, more than 40 percent attended college, and 15 percent of those had completed a graduate degree. Fourth, nearly two-thirds were self-employed. And, finally, 96 percent said they would want to be taught at home again. Knowles reported that they had many warm memories about their home schooling. Many mentioned the strong relationship it engendered with their parents, while others talked about the self-directed curriculum and individualized pace that a flexible program of home schooling permitted.

Yes, home schooling is a valid educational option, and socialization should not be an issue. After all, evidence of proper socialization is self-confidence.

How better to foster self-confidence than through the atmosphere of a loving home and the dedication of parents who are willing to invest their lives in their children."[19]

Gary Knowles also presented (along with K. de Olivares) a research paper entitled "Now we are adults: Attitudes, beliefs, and status of adults who were home-educated as children" at the 1990 Annual Meeting of the American Educational Research Association. Using surveys and life history techniques to study adults who were home educated, Knowles and de Olivares found that:

"these people grew up with advantages that contributed to their independent view of society and their role in it; they are not homogenous or amenable to easy categorization as a group, [those studied were] located throughout the U.S. and Canada in rural and urban areas, employed in a variety of professions and seem [sic] to be concentrated in occupations that allow for independence, flexibility, and/or creativity; they exhibit a wide range of political views and religious affiliations; a majority express a clearly positive attitude toward their home education and family experiences; they don't exhibit characteristics that suggest they are disadvantaged in any way as a result of their home education experience; they have no grossly negative perceptions of living in a pluralistic society; home schools may have advantages that have been unrecognized to this point." [20]

This important research informs us, among other things, that the majority of adults who were home schooled are "clearly positive" about their home schooling experience. This is a particularly telling point, because it may be presumed that these adults (with the benefit of added years, experience, and maturity) are considering the whole of their home schooling experience, and that experience surely includes the element of socialization.

1991 Research Studies: Hedin, Johnson, Kelley, & Kitchen

Hedin

Title: "A Study of the Self-Concept of Older Children in Selected Texas Churches Who Attend Home Schools as Compared to

Older Children Who Attend Christian Schools and Public Schools"

Author: Dr. Norma Hedin

According to an article in *The Teaching Home,*

> "Dr. Norma Hedin . . . examined the self-concept of home-educated children using the PHCSCS [Piers-Harris Children's Self-Concept Scale]. She only studied children from Baptist churches in Texas. She compared those who were educated in public, Christian, and home schools and found no difference in self-concept between these three groups. The self-concept of all of them as a group, however, was higher than that of the public school population."[21]

One of the reasons for Hedin's use of a sample base of children attending Baptist churches was because, as she explained, "It was assumed that children who attend the same church come from families who are somewhat similar in values, particularly spiritual values and educational values. Since these values could be consistent across the three groups, true differences in other areas could become more evident."[22] In the end, of course, Hedin found that "no statistically significant differences were found across school type, grade, or gender in the overall self-concept scores of older children in Texas Baptist churches."[23]

Finally, Hedin summed up her research study with the following statement:

> "The results of this study relate specifically to the claims of both proponents and opponents of home schools. *Using self-concept as a measure of socialization skills, it was evident that in this sample there were no significant differences in children's self-concept among*

the three educational settings under study [emphasis added]."[24]

Johnson

Title: "Socialization Practices of Christian Home School Educators in the State of Virginia"

Author: Dr. Kathie Carwile Johnson

Abstract of the Study

"The purpose of this study was to determine what practices home school educators in Virginia were using to meet the socialization needs of their middle school age students.

The researcher interviewed parents from ten home schooling families that were in the process of educating a middle school age child (11-14 years old). All parent respondents were from rural localities, encompassing five Virginia counties.

Previous research of socialization within the home school population has concentrated on general personal adjustment and self-esteem. In contrast, this study focused on seven areas of socialization: (1) personal identity, (2) personal destiny, (3) values and moral development, (4) autonomy, (5) relationships (peer and adult), (6) sexuality, and (7) social skills. These seven areas were used in a guided interview format to elicit information from the parents on practices that they had made a part of their instruction. Emergent issues related to socialization are included. Case studies were constructed on each of the ten families. A content analysis of the parent interviews, using the seven previously mentioned areas of socialization as categories, was completed.

The case studies, findings, conclusions and researcher remarks were limited to the study population. The researcher concluded from the data gathered that while home school educators were using many nontraditional methods, along with traditional methods, to address the socialization needs of their students, each area was being addressed. Findings indicated that the most important practices of these home school educators were those of: (1) parental modeling; (2) allowing the student to assume specific amounts of responsibility and to participate in situations usually reserved for much older students or adults; and, (3) instilling those values related to their Christian beliefs."[25]

Dr. Brian Ray summed up the essence of this research study on the NHERI website, noting that "Dr. Johnson (1991) concluded that home educators carefully address the socialization needs of their children in every area studied (i.e., personal identity, personal destiny, values and moral development, autonomy, relationships, sexuality, and social skills)."[26]

Johnson herself provides even more detail concerning her study in her article for the *Home School Researcher*, in which she reiterates her guiding research question ("what practices are home school educators using to meet the socialization needs of their middle school aged students?"[27]), and expands and clarifies her description of the seven areas of socialization addressed in her study, as follows:

"(a) Personal Identity (self esteem, solving the 'Who am I?' dilemma); (b) Personal Destiny (goals, achievement, career); (c) Values, Moral Development (accepting the rules and mores of society, self discipline, and learning problem solving strategies); (d) Autonomy (learning independence); (e) Relationships (peer attachment and adult friendships); (f) Sexuality (awareness of sex roles and physical changes); and (g) Social Skills (social rules, developing adult roles, acceptance of other's [sic] differences)."[28]

In conclusion, Johnson's findings indicated that every one of the above-noted areas of socialization was, indeed, being carefully addressed by the home schooling families.

Kelley

Title: "Socialization of Home Schooled Children: A Self-Concept Study"

Author: Dr. Steven W. Kelley

According to an article detailing his study in the *Home School Researcher*, Dr. Kelley

"examined the self-concept of home schooled children in 14 suburban Los Angeles cities.... The study focused on the self-concept of home schooled children in grades two through 10. The purposes of the study were to:

1. Address the 'bias' issue with regard to parents administering the self-concept scale in Taylor's 1986 study.
2. Examine the relationship between home schooling and the self-concept of home schooled children in suburban Los Angeles in grades two through 10.
3. Examine the differences between self-concept in home schooled children in suburban Los Angeles and the norms of self-concept in conventionally schooled children in grades four through 10. Grades two and three, however, could not be compared to conventionally schooled children because normative data for these grades are not available.
4. Examine the relationship between the self-concept of home schooled children in suburban Los Angeles and

various demographic factors. These factors included the following independent variables: age, grade-equivalence, gender, number of siblings, number of years in home school, socioeconomic status, prior attendance at a public school, number of children home schooled in the family, and operator educational level."[29]

In order to avoid the same question of possible bias that arose in the Taylor's study (because parents had administered the instrument to their own children), Kelley administered the PHCSCS [Piers-Harris Children's Self-Concept Scale] himself.[30] The results of Kelley's study indicated that "the self-concept of home schooling children in suburban Los Angeles was significantly higher . . . than the norms of conventionally schooled children on the global scale of the PHCSCS." He also noted that "the findings in this study [Kelley's study] are similar to John Taylor's (1986) findings. Taylor also found the self-concept of home schooled children to be significantly higher . . . than the norms of conventionally schooled children." Apparently, Kelley concluded, "It would appear that it makes no difference who administers the PHCSC."[31]

Another helpful summation of this particular research was provided by Dr. Brian Ray in *The Teaching Home*, when he noted that Kelley's study found that

> '*The self-concept of home schooling children in suburban Los Angeles was significantly higher . . . than the norms of conventionally schooled children* [emphasis added]. ... A low anxiety level could be a contributing factor. ... More contact with significant others, parental love, support and involvement, peer independence, and a sense of responsibility and self-worth may be other contributing factors."[32]

Kitchen

<u>Title:</u> "Socialization of Home School Children Versus Conventional School Children"

<u>Author:</u> Dr. Paul Kitchen

The purpose of Dr. Kitchen's study was to answer the question, "Are home schooled children advantaged or disadvantaged in their social adaptation/self-esteem by being educated at home?" And, in order to ascertain the answers to this question, Kitchen chose to use the "Self-Esteem Index," (rather than the Piers-Harris Children's Self-Concept Scale) as a research tool.[33]

Before "jumping" into the research process with assumptions about the measurement of self-concept, however, Kitchen asked the question, "Is self-concept a reflector of socialization?"[34] He then answers the question himself quite ably by drawing upon some extant research in this area, as is evidenced in the following discussion:

> "Purkey (1970) reported that the way children react to people, tasks and roles is often consistent with their view of self. Later, DeFrancesco and Taylor (1985) conducted a study on self-concept in middle school students where they found, ' ... what a person believes about himself affects what he does, what he sees and hears, and his capacity to cope with the environment' (p. 99)
>
> The views of these researchers is [sic] congruent with Cooley's (1902) theory of the Looking Glass Self. This theory has been the cornerstone concept in the development of research into socialization. It also plays an important role in the sociological conceptualization of self-concept. Briefly stated, the Looking Glass Self refers to the idea that we look to significant others in our lives in order to understand how they see us, and then in turn

we build our self-concept and self-esteem from the reflection of ourselves that we see from the[m].

Gecas and Swalbe (1983) followed up on this Looking Glass Self theory and strengthened the tie between self-concept and socialization. .... It would appear that the ability to successfully cope with one's environment is intricately connected with one's self-esteem."[35]

Clearly, then, self-concept may be seen as an appropriate indicator for measuring socialization.

Kitchen measured three different groups of children in his research study — home, private, and public schooled children. However, "due to the small number of responses from the public school group . . . the private and public school results were combined to form one category called Conventional schooled children."[36]

Of the four subscales measured by the Self-Esteem Index (Perception of Personal Security, Perception of Peer Popularity, Perception of Academic Competence, and Perception of Familiar Acceptance), home schooled children surpassed their conventionally schooled counterparts in all but one. Specifically, Kitchen found that "in three categories, Personal Security, Academic Competence, and Familial Acceptance, the home schooled group had higher percentages of children that scored above average as compared to the conventionally schooled children."[37] So, the only area in which the home schooled children *did not* exceed the conventionally schooled children was in the area of Perception of Peer Popularity.

Finally, one of the most interesting of Kitchen's findings has to do with the home schooled group's lower ranking in the Peer Popularity subscale. Kitchen notes that there is "an inverse relationship between self-esteem and peer popularity. This indicates that with a rise in Peer popularity there is a negative effect on overall self-esteem." He also notes that "it is only a moderate correlation, but certainly one that can't be ignored." [38]

1992 Research Studies: Shyers, Smedley, & Stough

Shyers

Title: "Comparison of Social Adjustment Between Home and Traditionally Schooled Students"

Author: Dr. Larry E. Shyers

Abstract of the Study

"Traditional schools provide for regular classroom contact with children of the same age, and it is assumed that this regular contact with other children aids appropriate social adjustment. By their very nature, home schools do not provide for regular formal classroom contact with children other than siblings. Because of this obvious difference, parents, educators, legislators, and courts have questioned whether children schooled at home are as socially well adjusted as their agemates in traditional programs. Investigation of this possible difference was the focus of this study.

This study compared the social adjustment of 70 children educated at home with that of 70 children educated in a traditional school setting. Three correlates of social adjustment were identified through a review of the literature: self-concept, behavior, and assertiveness. Each was assessed in children of both populations.

The results of this study imply that children between the ages of 8 and 10 have similar beliefs about themselves regardless of how they are schooled. All age groups in both research populations had self-concept scores higher than the national average as measured by the Piers-Harris Children's Self-Concept Scale.

The results of this study further indicate that children from both schooling environments participating in this study achieved scores on the Children's Assertive Behavior Scale revealing slightly passive understanding of social situations.

According to the results of this study, children between the ages of 8 and 10 who had been educated entirely in a home school had significantly fewer problem behaviors, as measured by the Direct Observation Form of the Child Behavior Checklist, than children of the same age from traditional schools. Children of this age in this study, who had been educated entirely in traditional schools, revealed problem behaviors above the normal range for national populations of the same age.

It can be concluded from the results of this study that appropriate social skills can develop apart from formal contact with children other than siblings. This supports the belief held by home school proponents."[39]

In a similarly titled article for the *Home School Researcher*, Shyers reiterates the basics of the above study, including the selection and purpose of the three different research instruments utilized: "The *Children's Assertive Behavior Scale* (CABS) . . . was chosen to assess knowledge of appropriate assertive responses," "the *Piers-Harris Children's Self Concept Scale* (PHCSCS) was chosen to measure a child's self-concept and feelings of social comfort," and "the *Direct Observation Form* (DOF) . . . was chosen to record the children's observed behaviors by trained observers."[40]

And what, specifically, did these three instruments tell us about the socialization of the home schooled and traditionally schooled children? Shyers provides the details of his findings in the following excerpt:

"The results of the data analysis indicated that both groups of children received scores on the *PHCSCS* that were above the national average. .... Both groups of children received raw scores on the *CABS* that were indications that they choose slightly passive responses to social situations. .... Neither group, however, received mean assertive scores that could be considered "very passive."

The most significant results of this study were found in actual observed behaviors. The *DOF* records problems behaviors by type and frequency. Home schooled students received significantly lower problem behavior scores than did their agemates from traditional program[s]. Although the problem behavior scores received by the traditional students in this study were above the national average according to the authors of the *DOF*, none of the observers felt the behaviors they observed were atypical for the age and gender of the subjects."[41]

Shyers goes on to suggest that one of the reasons for the differences in observed behavior may lie in the fact that

"it is reasonable to expect that children will imitate the behaviors that they observe most often. Traditionally schooled children spend an average of seven hours per weekday over a nine month period in the presence of other children and few adults. It would seem then, that their behaviors would most often reflect those of the majority of the children with whom they associate. In the case of this study, it was observed that traditionally schooled children tended to be considerably more aggressive, loud, and competitive than were the home schooled children of the same age.

In the case of the home schooled children, most of their day is spent with their parents and very few children. The primary models for behavior, therefore, are adults. Based on the social learning theory that children learn by imitating the behaviors of people whom they observe, home schooled children would thus most likely imitate the behaviors of their parents. The home schooled children in this study tended to be quiet, nonaggressive, and noncompetitive. Each child appeared to make up his or her own mind on how to behave.

The results of this study, therefore, draw into question the conclusions made by many educators and courts that traditionally educated children are more socially well adjusted than are those who are home schooled . . . ."[42]

One of the most interesting aspects of this study, and one that certainly bears repeating, is the fact that -- according to Samuel L. Blumenfeld -- "when Dr. Shyers started the study . . . he believed that the social adjustment of the homeschoolers would be far worse than that of the traditionally schooled, and he expected that this research would confirm that. But the results proved him wrong."[43] It's comforting to realize that even when researchers presume a certain outcome in a study, the data gathered will nevertheless tell its own story -- regardless of any personal presuppositions.

Smedley

Title:" Socialization of Home School Children"

Author: Thomas C. Smedley

In an article entitled "Research News: The Question of Socialization," home school researcher Dr. Brian Ray outlines the essence of Smedley's study, noting that

> "Thomas Smedley used the *Vineland Adaptive Behavior Scales* to evaluate the communication skills, socialization, and daily living skills of demographically matched public schooled and home-educated students. The data revealed that 'the home-educated children in this sample were significantly better socialized and more

mature than those in public school.' 'The immediate implication is that home-school families are providing adequately for socialization needs.'"[44]

In his own article detailing his 1992 study, Smedley illuminates the fact that "no researcher up to this point has investigated the home school socialization issue from a communication perspective." In his attempt to do just that, Smedley measured the social maturity of home schooled students, and then compared the results "to a demographically matched sample of public school students."[45]

In summing up the results of his research study, Smedley points out that

> *"The findings of this study indicate that children kept home are more mature and better socialized than those who are sent to school* [emphasis added]. The . . . population matches the demo-graphics of the national survey (Ray, 1990) fairly closely in terms of observed racial, professional, and religious characteristics. The public school students surveyed attend well-funded and well-staffed middle class schools. The public school students even share the religious values of the home school children. Yet, the socialization difference is there."[46]

Certainly one of the most important elements of this particular study is the fact that the research populations were matched demographically. In other words, those favorable elements often cited as essential for "good socialization" were present in both the home schooled and public schooled children, and *still* the home educated students were found to be "more mature and better socialized."

Stough

Title: "Social and Emotional States of Home Schooled Children and Conventionally Schooled Children in West Virginia"

Author: Lee Stough

Abstract of the Study

"This study compared home-schooled children to conventionally schooled children in West Virginia. A total of 30 home schooling families and 32 conventionally schooling families with children of 7 to 14 years of age participated in the study. The Vineland Adaptive Behavior Scales Classroom Edition was used to gather parent perspectives on the social sufficiency of their children. The children's self-evaluations were recorded on the Piers-Harris Children's Self-Concept Scale. A projective instrument, the Kinetic Drawing System for Family and School, was used to explore child-family-school interaction patterns for evidence of emotional indicators. *Results showed no statistical difference between home-schooled and conventionally schooled children in terms of social sufficiency, self-concept, or presence of emotional indicators* [emphasis added]. A reference list of 45 items is included."[47]

The findings presented in this abstract speak for themselves.

1993 Research Study: Burns

Title: "A Profile of Selected Characteristics of Arizona's Home Schooling Families"

Author: Dr. Patrick C. Burns

Abstract of the Study

"The purpose of this study was to profile selected characteristics of Arizona's home schooling families and describe the major reasons these families choose to school their children at home. Characteristics of home schooling families examined in the study were demographics, religious preference and commitment, educational philosophy and beliefs, and political and social beliefs. Responses were obtained from a survey of 425 families and personal interviews of 15 families. Many of the survey questions were comparable to questions from national opinion polls and the 1990 Arizona Census Report. This allowed comparisons of Arizona home schooling families with larger populations. The typical home schooling family in Arizona is a white two-parent family. Family income and level of educational attainment of home schoolers are higher than Arizona's adult population. A much greater percentage of home schoolers are employed in professional/managerial occupations. Most home schoolers identified themselves as Christian, Protestant, Baptist, or non-denominational. Religious commitment and church attendance are noticeably higher than the national population. Home schoolers expressed less support for government influence in education and demonstrated considerably less confidence in the public schools than the general population. They believe their method of education is superior to the public schools, because it provides the child individual attention in a family-centered environment, one-on-one instruction, and a curriculum that stresses the beliefs, values, and morals of the parents. While a sample of the national population demonstrated no clear political viewpoint or political party preference, Arizona's home schooling families are predominately Republican and conservative. Home schoolers exhibited considerably less confidence in America's major social institutions as compared to a sample of the national population. Home schooling families cited a number of reasons for deciding to teach their children at home. The most important reasons are to instill proper morals and values. *Other factors that influenced the decision to home school are family unity, ability to provide a better education, an opportunity to provide a better environment for socialization, and religious reasons* [emphasis added]."[48]

This is another study whose primary research focus was not socialization, but which nevertheless yielded results of some interest to us. According to Dr. Burns's findings, socialization is actually one of the reasons that parents choose to home school their children. In other words, far from being a negative issue of some concern, these parents perceived the socialization choices available to them in home schooling as a very positive aspect of their educational choice.

1994 Research Studies: Chatham-Carpenter, Lee, & Medlin

Chatham-Carpenter

Title: "Home vs. Public Schoolers: Differing Social Opportunities"

Author: Dr. April Chatham-Carpenter

In her study, Chatham-Carpenter posed three research questions:

(a) "Is there a significant difference in the size of home and public schooled subjects' social networks?"; (b) "are there significant differences between home and public schooled subjects for frequency of interaction with contacts?"; and (c) "are there significant differences between home and public subjects on reported closeness of relationships overall?"[49]

Using a pool of 21 home schooled adolescents and 20 publicly schooled adolescents from central Oklahoma, Chatham-Carpenter asked each subject to

> "keep a record of his/her interactions (interactions lasting at least 2 minutes or more) over a month's period of time (i.e., who s/he talked to and what s/he talked about to each person recorded). .... After the month was completed, each subject was asked to have his/her parents review the list and add any additional person with whom the subject usually interacted at least once a month. .... After the network list was constructed, follow-up survey forms ... were given to the subject to gain information about the subject's social contacts on the network list."[50]

After reviewing her findings, Chatham-Carpenter concluded that *"this study found that home schoolers are not 'at risk" socially (as compared to a similar group of public schoolers) in terms of the total numbers of people with whom they interact* [emphasis added]." Chatham-Carpenter also noted, almost as if in warning, that her study "demonstrates that the home schooling process does indeed affect the nature of the relationships experienced in adolescence for home schoolers."[51] The vast majority of home schooling parents, of course, would regard this as a highly positive finding.

Lee

Title: "The Socialization of Home-Schooled and Public-Schooled Children"

Author: Dr. Walter J. Lee

Abstract of the Study

"The purpose of this study was to determine whether home school or public school settings best fostered positive student socialization. A second purpose was to determine to what degree student socialization was affected by instructional time at school, and by parent time at home. Procedure. The Self-Perception Profile for Children (Harter, 1985) and the Adaptive Behavior Inventory for Children (ABIC) (Mercer & Lewis, 1982) were given to 61 students, ranging from 9 to 11 years old. Parents and teachers reported the amount of individual time they spent with students during instructional and non-instructional activities. Findings. No significant differences were found in non-instructional time, self-esteem scores, or in ABIC subscales of: peer relations, nonacademic schools roles, earner/ consumer, and self-maintenance. No significant correlations existed between self-esteem and instructional or non-instructional time spent with children. Students in home schools, however, scored significantly higher in the family, community, and average scores of the ABIC, and home school parents spent more time instructing students. A significant positive correlation was found between the ABIC family subscale and teacher instructional time. Conclusions. A larger sample could show more significant differences. Self-esteem is affected by factors not measured in this study. *Concerns regarding home schooling deficiencies are not warranted. Socialization of children in home schools is effective without exposure to large groups of children, and is more related to instructional time than non-instructional time. Home school parents are imparting positive family socialization, which is not inferior to the public school culture* [emphasis added]. Recommendation. Public school officials should be less concerned about student self-esteem in home schools, and objective measures are recommended if social development is a concern. An individual teaching style is recommended in public schools. Parents of public school children should supplement their child's education by giving instruction in the home. Communication between public school personnel and home schools should increase to better understand differences, and for a smoother transition from one setting to the other."[52]

As noted in the above abstract, Lee found in his research that the socialization received by home schooled children was "positive," and not "inferior" to the socialization received by those attending public schools. Lee also states, rather strongly, that "concerns regarding home schooling deficiencies are not warranted," and that officials in the public schools "should be less concerned" about the issue.

Medlin

Title: "Predictors of Academic Achievement in Home Educated Children: Aptitude, Self-Concept, and Pedagogical Practices"

Author: Dr. Richard G. Medlin

According to Dr. Medlin, in this research study

"home educated children's scholastic aptitude, educational self-concept, and their parents' teaching practices were examined to determine which combination of variables best predicted academic achievement. Thirty-six home schooled children and their parents—27 families in all—participated in this study.
Academic achievement was best predicted by scholastic aptitude, and the relationship between these two variables was quite strong. However, achievement scores were higher than aptitude scores, indicating that

ability alone could not explain the level of achievement observed. *These results suggest that the superior achievement often found among home schooled children is not due simply to higher native intelligence within that group . . . . Educational self-concept was high and was also a predictor of achievement* [emphasis added] , particularly for older children.[53]

Overall, this research demonstrated that although the scholastic aptitude of home schooled children was near average, they performed better than average in achievement and had a healthy academic self-concept."[54]

This is yet another highly interesting research study, because not only do the findings reveal that home schooled children have a "high" and "healthy" educational self-concept, but they also reveal the connection between educational self-concept and achievement. This connection is such a strong one, evidently, that a child's natural aptitude is not necessarily the primary predictor of educational success. In other words, Medlin found in this research study that home schooled children had such a healthy educational self-concept that their achievement "outpaced" even their natural aptitude, or, as he put it in his abstract, the "results suggest that the superior achievement often found among home schooled children is not due simply to higher native intelligence within that group . . . . Educational self-concept was high and was also a predictor of achievement."

1995 Research Study: Tillman

Title: "Home Schoolers, Self-Esteem, and Socialization"

Author: Vicki D. Tillman

According to Tillman,

"this study used a combination of questionnaire, self-report, and interview to describe home schooling socialization philosophy and practices, and looked at how home schooled pre- and early-adolescents fared in self-esteem. The questionnaire collected data on types and frequencies of outside-the-family socialization opportunities for home schoolers. The 11- to 14-year-olds were administered the *Self-Esteem Index* to compare their self-esteem scores with the norms. Interviews were conducted with five families to give them, in-depth, the opportunity to share their personal philosophies toward home schooling and socialization and self-esteem."[55] The results of the study indicated that "scores in all five scales of the *SEI* [Self-Esteem Index] are above the norms."[56]

Dr. Brian Ray offers the following helpful synopsis of Tillman's research, noting that the findings

"show that these home schoolers are not isolated, but active, contributing members of society, even in childhood. Ninety-eight percent are involved in weekly church meetings and other activities which require interfacing with various ages and settings... [emphasis added]. As rated by the Self-Esteem Index (SEI), these home schoolers have above-average self-esteem."[57]

1996 Research Study: Breshears

Title: "Characteristics of Home Schools and Home School Families in Idaho"

Author: Dr. Shirley M. Breshears

Abstract of the Study

"The purpose of this study was to provide information about the characteristics of Idaho home schools, home school families and the opinions of those families concerning their home schools. A 30-item questionnaire was mailed to 250 randomly selected members of Idaho Home Educators. The data was analyzed and summarized using descriptive statistics and is presented in narrative format. The results of this study indicate that in home school families in Idaho the mother is usually the teacher, both parents are in the 30-40 age group, 50% of the mothers do not work outside the home, the family has an average of three children, the average annual income is $40,000.00, the parent has an average of two years of college, 99% of the families attend religious services on a regular basis, the home school child watches television an average of 1.15 hours per day, they go to the public library on a regular basis, and 75% of the parents read aloud every day to their children. Parents' primary reasons for establishing a home school were to provide the best possible education for their children and to teach family values and morals which are Bible-based and God-centered. Curriculum materials were described as being selected to enforce these values. Over 80% of the families reported being influenced by peers, home school organizations, or their churches to begin home schooling. *Socialization was 'not an issue' for 26% of the families; the remaining 74% stated they socialize with family, friends, club groups, home school support groups, and neighborhood children* [emphasis added]. The greatest satisfaction derived from home schooling was reported to be a close-knit family unit; the hardest thing to accomplish was reported to be time management. Thirty-seven percent of the home school families planned to take advantage of Section 33-203 in Idaho Code concerning dual enrollment which allows them to attend public school for selected classes. Ninety-two percent of the home school families planned to continue to educate their children at home the following year. Seventy-six percent had operated a home school for five years or less and 24% had been teaching their children for six years or more. Sixty-four percent planned to continue to teach at home until the children finished high school. Reading/English, Math and the Bible were most emphasized in the Idaho home schools and many publishers were used when selecting the curriculum. Fifty-three percent of the families reported having over 200 books in their libraries. Only about 15% of the families were operating a cottage industry. Based on the findings of this study implications for further study are included."[58]

According to the results of this study, then, 26% of the home schooling families who participated felt that socialization was simply "not an issue," and the remaining 74% indicated that their children socialized with "family, friends, club groups, home school support groups, and neighborhood children."

Finally, one other result from this research study merits closer scrutiny here. Apparently, 36% of the home school parents Breshears studied

"said they were satisfied with home schooling because it allows the parent and child to develop a close relationship with includes being able to see the 'light go on' when the child catches on to a concept being taught. The comments related to the close parent/child relationship indicated *parents know they are meeting the child's social, spiritual, and educational needs in the best way possible*" [emphasis added]. [59]

1997 Research Study: Ray

<u>Title:</u> "Strengths of Their Own--Home Schoolers Across America: Academic Achievement, Family Characteristics, and Longitudinal Traits"

<u>Author:</u> Dr. Brian D. Ray

In this groundbreaking national study, Ray studied a number of important aspects and elements of home schooling and the home schooling community. Of chief importance to the theme of this book are Ray's findings regarding the issue of socialization, which are as follows:

> "Children in these families were engaged in a wide variety of social activities. For example, 87% engaged in play activities with people outside the family, 77% participated in Sunday school, 48% were involved in group sports, and 47% were involved in music classes. These children spent, on average, 10 hours per week in contact with non-family adults. It is clear, as other researchers have pointed out, that these children are not socially isolated. Further, it appears that the amount and quality of their social interaction does not inhibit their social and psychological development."[60]

Again, the research findings speak for themselves.

1998 Research Studies: Gray & Humphrey

Gray

Title: "A Study of the Academic Achievements of Home-Schooled Students Who Have Matriculated Into Postsecondary Institutions"

Author: Dr. Dovie W. Gray

Abstract of the Study

"Home-schooling is once again becoming a popular alternative for parents wanting to offer the best education for their children. This study investigated home-schooled students' academic achievement in post-secondary institutions by comparing their performance with that of students who had graduated from traditional public and private schools. The basis for comparison was freshman English grades, Scholastic Aptitude Test Scores, overall grade point averages, and demographic variables which included: age, gender, income, number of siblings, race, and college classification. The perceptions of home-schooled students and parents about home school programs were compared as well using selected questions to determine perceptions about socialization development skills of home-schooled students. The study consisted of 38 home-schooling parents, 56 home-schooled students, and 44 traditional students. Students attended universities/ colleges in the state of Georgia, and the average of both traditional students and home-schooled students was 18. Average household income was between $50,000--$99,000. T-tests were generated to determine if there were significant differences between home-school students' and traditional students' SAT scores and freshman English grades. Findings indicated that there were no significant differences between the two groups. Overall the study suggested that home-schooled students demonstrated similar academic achievement in college as students who had attended traditional universities/colleges."[61]

The most significant finding of this study--again, insofar as the purpose of this book is concerned--is that both academic and socialization elements of the traditionally schooled and the home schooled were compared, and that the "findings indicated that there were no significant differences between the two groups."

Humphrey

Title: "Why Parents Choose to Home School Their Children: A Qualitative Perspective of Mothers Who Are Members of Home School Support Groups"

Author: Dr. Elmer H. Humphrey

Abstract of the Study

"Home schooling has become a viable option for many parents dissatisfied with public or private education. The major reasons to home school include academics, socialization, religious, family, and safety. Parents who home school for academic reasons like the flexibility available with home schooling. Parents can teach their child according to the learning style that their child learns best. Parents are also able to pace the rate of the curriculum to meet the individual needs of each child. If a child needs extra time to master an objective, or if a child is capable of moving at a quicker pace, this can be accommodated. Parents who home schooled have additional opportunities to pursue the child's individual interests. *Parents who home school like the ability to avoid negative socialization. Name calling, negative influences, and peer dependence can be decreased as a result of home schooling. Home schooling parents feel that their children have the opportunity to make friends with diverse age groups. Parents believe the real world is made up of socialization in multiple-age groups, not peer dependent age groups* [emphasis added]. Some home school parents are concerned that the public schools systematically excludes religion, especially Christianity, from the public school agenda. Parents who home school for religious reasons, like the ability to integrate their religious values with the daily curriculum. Safety is a relatively new area of choosing home schooling. Some parents are not assured that if they send their children to public school they will be safe. Home schooling is providing a viable alternative for some parents. Parents need to be cautioned that home schooling needs to be researched before embracing it whole heartedly [sic]. Drawbacks to home schooling could include: financial decrease due to single income, time demands on the home school teachers, and opposition from relatives and friends."[62]

Dr. Humphrey's findings concerning socialization (parents feel that home schooling provides the opportunity to avoid negative socialization, etc.), are very much in keeping with the findings of other researchers, and are also in line with many of the opinions expressed by home schoolers themselves in Chapter II ("Voices From the Front").

1999 Research Studies: Francis

Title: "Social Skill of Home Schooled and Conventionally Schooled Children: A Comparison Study"

Author: Dr. David J. Francis

Abstract of the Study

"Despite opposition from many local school boards and various educational groups, home schooling continues to be a growing trend across the nation (Holtrop, 1996; Mayberry, 1989; Ray, 1996, 1997; Ritter, 1997). As this population grows, concerns abound regarding the effects home schooling may have on the socialization of these children (Murray, 1996). The articles in this area of research are varied in methodology and theoretical orientation when measuring the socialization construct. Moreover, few studies have addressed the socialization of home schooled children with more appropriate measures of social behavior. The purpose of this study was to examine the socialization of home schooled children in relation to conventionally schooled children (i.e., public or private). Exploring the socialization domain was accomplished by examining parents' perceptions of matched groups of home and conventionally educated children in rural western New York."[63]

What were the findings and conclusions of Francis's study? According to the *Home Centered Learning Annotated Bibliography*, Francis's study

"investigated whether home educated children's social skills differed from the social skills of a matched comparison group of conventionally educated children. . . . The results from this study indicate that the home schooled children earned higher social skill standard scores, and self-control scores than their conventionally educated peers. These differences in total social skills and self-control scores, were also found following the removal of five methodologically questionable subject pairs. *These findings suggest that home schooling has a significant positive effect on children's social skills*" [emphasis added].[64]

Evidently, even though Dr. Francis found the "methodology and theoretical orientation" of former studies of home schooling to be less than "appropriate" (as stated in his abstract), his own study utilizing his own methodology nevertheless resulted in highly positive findings, specifically, "that home schooling has a significant positive effect on children's social skills."

Discussion

Looking at the history of home schooling socialization research is an undertaking at once rewarding and fascinating, as the "building" or "platform" process in the research becomes readily apparent. Studying the studies themselves, it is easy to see how one study builds upon another in a variety of ways (e.g., by replicating the study, expanding upon it, correcting perceived methodological problems in the original study, or deeming the original study to be inadequate and/or inappropriate and proceeding in an entirely different direction).

When considering only those studies whose research was aimed primarily at the socialization aspect of home schooling, it is easy to discern how subsequent studies used Dr. John W. Taylor's original 1986 study as a reference point for their own research. Indeed, in Dr. Kathie Johnson's 1991 study, she notes in her abstract that

> "previous research of socialization within the home school population has concentrated on general personal adjustment and self-esteem [at this point in the research history, she clearly refers here to Taylor's study]. In contrast, this study focused on seven areas of socialization."[65]

Also in 1991, Dr. Steven Kelley made the methodology of Taylor's original study an element of his own research by consciously setting about to "address the 'bias' issue with regard to parents administering the self-concept scale in Taylor's 1986 study."[66] After making the necessary adjustments to correct this potential bias and evaluating his own findings, Kelley came to the conclusion that "it would appear that it makes no difference who administers the PHCSC [the research tool used in both Taylor's and Kelley's study]."[67]

Dr. Paul Kitchen (also in 1991), decided to investigate the socialization of home schooled children by, again, determining their levels of self-esteem/self-concept. Unlike Taylor (who used the Piers-Harris Children's Self-Concept Scale), Kitchen chose to work with the "Self-Esteem Index" as his research tool. And -- given the lengthy and detailed discussion of the issue in his research article -- Kitchen was also apparently concerned about the theoretical assumptions and constructs which regard self-concept as an indicator of socialization. He asked, "Is self-concept a reflector of socialization?"[68] and he answered the question (with appropriate research) to his own satisfaction, with a positive response.

This concern about the use of self-concept and/or self-esteem as an indicator of socialization is an ongoing one, and one which Taylor himself may well have foreseen, as he notes in his own abstract that *"insofar as self-concept is a reflector of socialization* [emphasis added], it appears that few homeschoolers are socially deprived."[69] In fact, as we have seen thus far in this study, many researchers clearly consider self-concept to be a valid measure of socialization, while other argue that "the constructs of self-esteem and self-concept . . . are insufficient indicators of social behavior."[70] Such differences of opinion should be welcomed, as they insure a healthy and vigorous debate and continuing, ever-broadening research.

Dr. Larry Shyers's landmark 1992 study expanded upon the use of self-concept as a measure of socialization, by measuring not only the self-concept of home schooled children, but their behavior and assertiveness levels as well. Thomas Smedley (1992) used a different theoretical construct for his research altogether, noting that "no researcher up to this point has investigated the home school socialization issue from a communication perspective."[71] And Lee Stough, also in 1992, investigated socialization not only with the Piers-Harris Children's Self-Concept Scale, but also with the Vineland Adaptive Behavior Scales and the Kinetic Drawing System.

In 1994, Dr. Walter Lee implemented both the Self-Perception Profile for Children and the Adaptive Behavior Inventory for Children into his research. The following year, Dr. Vicki Tillman used "a combination of questionnaire, self-report, and interview to describe home schooling socialization philosophy and practices,"[72] and also administered the Self-Esteem Index to her research participants. In 1999, Dr. David Francis eschewed the use of self-concept as an indicator altogether, choosing instead to focus on the measurement of social skills and self-control.

Looking back at this research history and its starting point (with self-concept as an indicator of socialization), it becomes clear that while many researchers still utilized self-concept measured in one form or another as at least one indicator of socialization, they began to deliberately and carefully add additional research tools and constructs to their studies. Other researchers, as we have seen, purposely conducted their research without the use of self-concept as a socialization construct. It is also worth noting that as the research progressed, it seemed that no researcher appeared to be satisfied with simply administering one scale/test/form/research tool. This is an entirely wonderful and logical development in the research, because the more aspects of socialization that are measured -- with different tools and by different researchers with different methodologies and constructs -- the better.

Conclusions

Even more fascinating than the examination of home schooling socialization research studies are their remarkably consistent findings, because – despite the often vast differences in methodologies and research constructs utilized – they are all positive.

But let us be more specific. The findings of the research studies examined in this chapter may be divided into three distinct categories, each of which has positive ramifications for the home schooling family. Into the first category fall those findings which indicate that (a) socialization is not considered a problem by home schooling families, (b) home schooling families provide ample opportunities for social interaction outside the home, and (c) socialization concerns are one of the reasons that parents decided to home school their children.

The second category contains all the findings that indicate that there is no statistical difference in measured socialization indicators between home schooled children and conventionally schooled (i.e., publicly or privately schooled) children. In other words, according to these studies, home schooled children are at least as well socialized as their conventionally schooled counterparts. Into the third and final category go all the research findings that indicate that home schooled children are actually better socialized than their conventionally schooled counterparts.

In sum -- when comparing home schooled children to conventionally schooled children -- the results of these research studies may be summed up as follows: *At best, home schooled children are better socialized than conventionally schooled children; at worst, they are at least as well socialized as conventionally schooled children.* This is the kind of solid, research-based conclusion that should effectively silence any and all opposition. Sadly, however, it doesn't, as we shall see in the following chapter.

Endnotes – Chapter III

[1] Schemmer, B. A. S. (1985). *Case studies of four families engaged in home education.* Unpublished Doctoral Dissertation, Ball State University (# AAT 8525190).

[2] (p. 8). Ray, B. D. (1987). On case studies of four families engaged in home education by Beverly Schemmer (a review). *Home School Researcher, 3* (1), 5-10.

[3] (p. 9). Ray, B. D. (1987). On case studies of four families engaged in home education by Beverly Schemmer (a review). *Home School Researcher, 3* (1), 5-10.

[4] Delahooke, M. M. (1986). *Home educated children's social/emotional adjustment and academic achievement: A comparative study.* Unpublished Doctoral Dissertation, California School of Professional Psychology, Los Angeles (# 8608759).

[5] www.nheri.org (retrieved 6/22/01).

[6] (p. 35). Ray, B. D. (2000, Summer). Research news: The question of socialization. *The Teaching Home, 18* (2).

[7] Taylor, J. W. (1986). *Self-concept in home-schooling children.* Unpublished Doctoral Dissertation, Andrews University (# 8624219).

[8] www.nheri.org (retrieved 6/22/01).

[9] (p. 35). Ray, B. D. (2000, Summer). Research news: The question of socialization. *The Teaching Home, 18*(2).

[10] (p. 155). Ray, B. D. (2002). *Home centered learning annotated bibliography* (11th ed.). Salem, OR: NHERI.

[11] (p. 1). Wartes, J. (1987). Report from the 1986 homeschool testing and other descriptive information about Washington's homeschoolers: A summary. *Home School Researcher, 3* (1), 1-4.

[12] (pp. 3-4). Wartes, J. (1987). Report from the 1986 homeschool testing and other descriptive information about Washington's homeschoolers: A summary. *Home School Researcher, 3* (1), 1-4.

[13] Montgomery, L. R. (1989). *The effect of home schooling on the leadership skills of home schooled students.* Unpublished Doctoral Dissertation, Seattle University (# 8925349).

[14] www.nheri.org (retrieved 6/22/01).

[15] (p. 8). Montgomery, L. (1989). The effect of home schooling on the leadership skills of home schooled students. *Home School Researcher, 5* (1), 1-10.

[16] (p. 9). Montgomery, L. (1989). The effect of home schooling on the leadership skills of home schooled students. *Home School Researcher, 5* (1), 1-10.

[17] Beaven, C. C. (1990). *Living and learning: A phenomenological study of home education.* Unpublished Doctoral Dissertation, University of Michigan (# AAT 9034382).

[18] www.nheri.org (retrieved 6/22/01).

[19] Volume 18, Program 12; Airdate: January 18, 2000; Available: http://www.hslda.org

[20] (p. 72). Ray, B. D. (2002). *Home centered learning annotated bibliography* (11th ed.). Salem, OR: NHERI.

[21] (p. 35). Ray, B. D. (2000, Summer). Research news: The question of socialization. *The Teaching Home, 18* (2).

[22] (p. 1). Hedin, N. S. (1991). Self-concept of Baptist children in three educational settings. *Home School Researcher, 7* (3), 1-5.

[23] (p. 3). Hedin, N. S. (1991). Self-concept of Baptist children in three educational settings. *Home School Researcher, 7* (3), 1-5.

[24] (p. 3). Hedin, N. S. (1991). Self-concept of Baptist children in three educational settings. *Home School Researcher, 7* (3), 1-5.

[25] Johnson, K. C. (1991). *Socialization practices of Christian home school educators in the state of Virginia.* Unpublished Doctoral Dissertation, University of Virginia (#9131588).

[26] www.nheri.org (retrieved 6/22/01).

[27] (p. 9). Johnson, K. C. (1991). Socialization practices of Christian home school educators in the state of Virginia. *Home School Researcher, 7* (1), 9-16.

28 (p. 10). Johnson, K. C. (1991). Socialization practices of Christian home school educators in the state of Virginia. *Home School Researcher*, 7 (1), 9-16.

29 (pp. 1-2). Kelley, S. W. (1991). Socialization of home schooled children: A self-concept study. *Home School Researcher*, 7 (4), 1-12.

30 (p. 7). Kelley, S. W. (1991). Socialization of home schooled children: A self-concept study. *Home School Researcher*, 7 (4), 1-12.

31 (p. 9). Kelley, S. W. (1991). Socialization of home schooled children: A self-concept study. *Home School Researcher*, 7 (4), 1-12.

32 (p. 35). Ray, B. D. (2000, Summer). Research news: The question of socialization. *The Teaching Home*, 18 (2).

33 (p. 8). Kitchen, P. (1991). Socialization of home school children versus conventional school children. *Home School Researcher*, 7 (3), 7-13.

34 (p. 8). Kitchen, P. (1991). Socialization of home school children versus conventional school children. *Home School Researcher*, 7 (3), 7-13.

35 (pp. 8-9). Kitchen, P. (1991). Socialization of home school children versus conventional school children. *Home School Researcher*, 7 (3), 7-13.

36 (pp. 9-10). Kitchen, P. (1991). Socialization of home school children versus conventional school children. *Home School Researcher*, 7 (3), 7-13.

37 (p. 10). Kitchen, P. (1991). Socialization of home school children versus conventional school children. *Home School Researcher*, 7 (3), 7-13.

[38] (p. 11). Kitchen, P. (1991). Socialization of home school children versus conventional school children. *Home School Researcher, 7* (3), 7-13.

[39] Shyers, L. E. (1992). *Comparison of social adjustment between home and traditionally schooled students.* Unpublished Doctoral Dissertation, University of Florida, Gainesville (#9304052).

[40] (p. 2). Shyers, L. E. (1992). A comparison of social adjustment between home and traditionally schooled students. *Home School Researcher, 8* (3), 1-8.

[41] (p. 5). Shyers, L. E. (1992). A comparison of social adjustment between home and traditionally schooled students. *Home School Researcher, 8* (3), 1-8.

[42] (pp. 5-6). Shyers, L. E. (1992). A comparison of social adjustment between home and traditionally schooled students. *Home School Researcher, 8* (3), 1-8.

[43] (p. 71). Blumenfeld, S. L. (1998). *Homeschooling: A parents guide to teaching children.* Secaucus, NJ: Citadel Press.

[44] (p. 35). Ray, B. D. (2000, Summer). Research news: The question of socialization. *The Teaching Home, 18* (2).

[45] (p. 9). Smedley, T. C. (1992). Socialization of home school children. *Home School Researcher, 8* (3), 9-16.

[46] (p. 12). Smedley, T. C. (1992). Socialization of home school children. *Home School Researcher, 8* (3), 9-16.

[47] Stough, L. (1992). *Social and emotional states of home schooled children and conventionally schooled children in West Virginia.* Unpublished Master's Thesis, University of West Virginia (ERIC Document Reproduction Service No. ED 353 079).

[48] Burns, P. C. (1993). *A profile of selected characteristics of Arizona's home schooling families.* Unpublished Doctoral Dissertation, Northern Arizona University (#AAT 9416229).

[49] (p. 16). Chatham-Carpenter, A. (1994). Home vs. public schoolers: Differing social opportunities. *Home School Researcher,* 10 (1), 15-24.

[50] (p. 16). Chatham-Carpenter, A. (1994). Home vs. public schoolers: Differing social opportunities. *Home School Researcher,* 10 (1), 15-24.

[51] (p. 21). Chatham-Carpenter, A. (1994). Home vs. public schoolers: Differing social opportunities. *Home School Researcher,* 10 (1), 15-24.

[52] Lee, W. J. (1994). *The socialization of home-schooled and public-schooled children.* Unpublished Doctoral Dissertation, University of La Verne (#AAT 9512212).

[53] (p. 4). Medlin, R. G. (1994). Predictors of academic achievement in home educated children: Aptitude, self-concept, and pedagogical practices. *Home School Researcher,* 10 (3), 1-7.

[54] (p. 5). Medlin, R. G. (1994). Predictors of academic achievement in home educated children: Aptitude, self-concept, and pedagogical practices. *Home School Researcher,* 10 (3), 1-7.

[55] (p. 2). Tillman, V. D. (1995). Home schoolers, self-esteem, and socialization. *Home School Researcher,* 11 (3), 1-6.

[56] (p. 5). Tillman, V. D. (1995). Home schoolers, self-esteem, and socialization. *Home School Researcher,* 11 (3), 1-6.

[57] (p. 35). Ray, B. D. (2000, Summer). Research news: The question of socialization. *The Teaching Home,* 18(2).

[58] Breshears, S. M. (1996). *Characteristics of home schools and home school families in Idaho.* Unpublished Doctoral Dissertation, University of Idaho (#AAT 9629157).

[59] (p. 19). Ray, B. D. (2002). *Home centered learning annotated bibliography* (11th ed.). Salem, OR: NHERI.

[60] (pp. 77-78). Ray, B. D. (1997). *Strengths of their own--Home schoolers across America: Academic achievement, family characteristics, and longitudinal traits.* Salem, OR: NHERI.

[61] Gray, D. W. (1998). *A study of the academic achievements of home-schooled students who have matriculated into postsecondary institutions.* Unpublished Doctoral Dissertation, University of Sarasota (#AAT9825584).

[62] Humphrey, E. H. (1998). *Why parents choose to home school their children: A qualitative perspective of mothers who are members of home school support groups.* Unpublished Doctoral Dissertation, Saint Louis University (#AAT9911951).

[63] Francis, D. J. (1999). *Social skills of home schooled and conventionally schooled children: A comparison study.* Unpublished Doctoral Dissertation, Alfred University (#AAT9962560).

[64] (p. 44). Ray, B. D. (2002) *Home centered learning annotated bibliography* (11th ed.). Salem, OR: NHERI.

[65] Johnson, K. C. (1991). *Socialization practices of Christian home school educators in the state of Virginia.* Unpublished Doctoral Dissertation, University of Virginia (#9131588).

[66] (p. 1). Kelley, S.W. (1991). Socialization of home schooled children: A self-concept study. *Home School Researcher, 7* (4), 1-12.

[67] (p. 9). Kelley, S.W. (1991). Socialization of home schooled children: A self-concept study. *Home School Researcher, 7* (4), 1-12.

[68] (p. 8). Kitchen, P. (1991). Socialization of home school children versus conventional school children. *Home School Researcher, 7* (3), 7-13.

[69] Taylor, J. W. (1986). *Self-concept in home-schooling children.* Unpublished Doctoral Dissertation, Andrews University (# 8624219).

[70] Francis, D. J., & Keith, T. Z. (2001). Self-esteem and home schooling socialization research: A work in progress. *Home School Researcher, 14* (3), 1-9.

[71] (p. 12). Smedley, T. C. (1992). Socialization of home school children. *Home School Researcher, 8* (3), 9-16.

[72] (p. 5). Tillman, V. D. (1995). Home schoolers, self-esteem, and socialization. *Home School Researcher, 11* (3), 1-6.

Chapter IV

Yes, But Doesn't the NEA Have Some Negative Things to Say About Home Schooling?

In a word, "yes." But let's take a look at the elements of their opposition, and the possible reasons behind it.

Before we go any further, however, I'd like to take a moment to share with you my genuine and unfeigned admiration for teachers in general and the teaching profession as a whole. I am both happy and proud to say that I come from a long line of public school educators and college professors, and it is my firm belief that teaching is an entirely honorable and noble calling.

That having been said, let me point out the obvious: In the world of education as in the world in general, things have changed quite a bit in the last several years. Attitudes and basic beliefs once taken for granted have changed drastically, and the foundations for and approaches to education have shifted dramatically as well. There are many fewer "givens" (as to issues of right and wrong, ethical behavior, discipline, etc.) in the educator's world than there used to be. As a result, I believe that being a public school teacher today is very likely a great deal more difficult than it was 50 or even 20 years ago. And, while I have heard real, documented horror stories about the attitudes and behaviors of some public school teachers, it must also be said that there are some wonderful, devoted, gifted, and caring teachers in the world of public education, and it is these teachers in particular that I applaud. Theirs is not an easy job.

And theirs is NOT the job home schoolers are attempting to do. Home schoolers are not attempting to teach 25-35 different students per day (or per hour in the higher grades) -- students with different learning styles, different educational backgrounds, and different aptitudes. To perform such a job effectively definitely requires a great deal of training.

It's simplistic but true. Comparing teaching in public and/or private schools to the teaching in home schooling must be likened to the old axiom of comparing apples and oranges -- very similar, and, at the same time, very different. Apples and oranges both fall into the larger category of "fruit," but they are obviously very different foods. In the same manner, both public/private school teaching and home schooling fall into the same broad category of "education," but one is dealing with education to the masses, and one is dealing with education within the family unit. The requirements to do each effectively are quite different. For example, home schooling parents don't need to know all the different kinds of learning styles in existence and how best to deal with each one--they only need to be familiar with those styles that directly affect their own children.

The Opposition of the National Education Association (NEA), and the Reasons Behind It

So, since teaching in the public schools and teaching your own children in a home school are so clearly and dramatically different, *why* does the NEA so vigorously oppose home schooling? And *how*, exactly, does it oppose home schooling?

How?

Let's address this last question first. Just *how* does the NEA set itself against the home schooling movement? Its first step is to adopt resolutions against it. Following is the NEA's home schooling resolution B-68, first adopted in 1988:

"The National Education Association believes that home schooling programs cannot provide the student with a comprehensive education experience. When home schooling occurs, students enrolled must meet all state requirements. Home schooling should be limited to the children of the immediate family, with all expenses being borne by the parents/guardians. Instruction should be by persons who are licensed by the appropriate state education licensure agency, and a curriculum approved by the state department of education should be used.

The Association also believes that home-schooled students should not participate in any extracurricular activities in the public schools.

The Association further believes that local public school systems should have the authority to determine grade placement and/or credits earned toward graduation for students entering or re-entering the public school setting from a home school setting." (1988, 2000)[1]

In "Decoding the NEA Resolutions," Phyllis Schlafly reports on details of the 1999 NEA conference and its activities, lobbying goals, and proposals. Under a section entitled "The NEA Will Work to--," Schlafly notes other stated goals of the NEA, including yet another anti-home schooling proposal, specifically: The NEA will work to "oppose tax-free IRA withdrawals for private and religious school and home-schooling expenses."[2]

Apparently, the NEA would like to exert control not only over the curriculum of the home schooled child (as found in its resolution concerning home schooling, that "a curriculum approved by the state department of education should be used") and the home school teacher's qualifications ("instruction should be by persons who are licensed by the appropriate state education licensure agency"), but also over the home school family's finances as well. This position is made quite clear in that the NEA opposes tax-free withdrawals for home schooling expenses, asserts that "all expenses" relevant to the home schooling process are to be "borne by the parents/ guardians," and believes "that home-schooled students should not participate in any extracurricular activities in the public schools."

This last assertion is particularly galling to families, as it is made despite the fact that home schooling parents are paying the same taxes to support public education as are other parents, and therefore they should logically be allowed the privilege of utilizing those services which they themselves help to fund. Ms. Schlafly reiterated this very same point when interviewed for *WorldNetDaily.com*: "The home-school parents are paying the same school taxes that the other schools' children's parents are paying. I see no reason why they can't enjoy some of the benefits of public schools if they are participating in the funding of these programs."[3] Ms. Schafly goes on to note the obvious: "This is part of their [the NEA's] effort to ostracize home-schoolers."[4]

But the adopting of resolutions and lobbying against the use of IRA funds for home schooling expenses are not the only elements of public education opposition. Despite the fact that home schooling is now legal in every state, local school districts can still initiate legal action against those families that choose to home school. One recent example is the suit filed by California's Berkeley Unified School District, which brought proceedings against four home schooling families.

According to the National Center for Policy Analysis, "The families were summoned to a truancy hearing at which they declined to provide attendance records or curriculum information, [and they were then] referred to the Alameda County District Attorney for contributing to the delinquency of minors."[5]

Even more alarming is that "legal observers warn these actions could be the first in a test case to outlaw home schooling in the state. But the teacher's unions and educational establishment bureaucrats are up against a [California] state code which doesn't even mention home schooling -- let alone prevent it."[6]

Unfortunately, California isn't the only state in which home schooling parents are involved in litigation as a result of their educational choice. Although, as was stated earlier, home schooling is officially legal in every state in the United States, some individual counties and school districts still make home schooling families defend their right to this educational alternative in court.

Clearly, the NEA has firmly and sometimes aggressively set itself against home schooling as an educational choice and home schooling parents as practitioners of that choice. Now that we have looked at some of the many ways the NEA opposes home schooling, let us now look at the remaining question of *why*? Why is the NEA so entirely and fervently negative about this issue?

Why?

I believe the answer to this question can be broken down into four very simple elements: Professional pride, control, money, and politics.

The issue of *professional pride* is certainly an easy one to understand. A public school teacher spends years in training in order to qualify for a teaching certificate, and--after that goal is achieved--attends regular in-service meetings and conferences to keep herself/himself up-to-date and informed about current educational trends and practices. This same public school teacher now sees the media flooded with stories about how home schooled children are besting public schooled children on a myriad of standardized tests and national competitions. And, for the most part, these home schooling parents aren't even certified, trained teachers!

Such very public revelations of the excellent academic performance of the majority of home schooled children are, I believe, something of an embarrassment to the public school teacher. Again, as mentioned earlier, teaching in home schooling and teaching in public schools are two very different creatures. Still, it's the public's perceptions that are most damaging to these professional educators. In a profession that for years has struggled for adequate respect--and the funding that follows such respect--the very excellent (and very public) academic performance of home schooled children is a harsh blow indeed.

Another reason for the NEA's opposition is *control*. What are home schooled children learning? Are they being exposed to the "correct" attitudes and approaches to the world and to society? What truths are they being taught? More importantly, *whose* truths are they being taught?

Actually, the issue of control is very closely linked to the issue of professional pride--how can untrained parents choose the best curriculum to teach their own children, and know the best ways in which to teach them? Surely, the professional educator reasons, such pedagogical decisions are best made by those who have had years of professional educational training.

Clearly—given the statements in the NEA's anti-home schooling resolution noted earlier--the NEA would like very much to control what home schooled children learn and how they learn it. One of the reasons for the NEA's opposition to home schooling, then, undoubtedly has to do with the simple fact that *they are not in control* of the curriculum content in the home school.

The next reason is also a very basic one – *money*. Public schools are allotted their funding based upon many different and often complicated policies and procedures. The most basic-- and the one most directly affected by home schoolers--is the "head count." How many students are in each classroom? How many seats are filled? The number of students attending a public school has a direct bearing on the amount of funding that school receives. So, in a very real way, the home schooling movement is "hitting" the public schools in another painful place—the pocketbook.

The last and final reason for the NEA's oftentimes vitriolic attack against the home schooling movement has to do with the issue of *politics*. The majority of home schooling families in the United States are both Christian in faith and conservative in political belief. [7] [8] (Although the last few years have likely seen an increase in the number of home schoolers who are neither of these things, it is nevertheless most probably true that the simple majority of home schoolers are both.[9]) So, how is this an element of the contention between the NEA and home schoolers?

In the most simple and basic of terms, home schoolers are (or at least are perceived to be) solidly conservative, and the leadership of the NEA is (although it should be noted, *not* all of its membership) solidly liberal. Two diametrically opposed factions. Right and Left.

The liberal beliefs, stances, and leanings of the NEA are a matter of public record. Indeed, a complaint was filed against the NEA because it "concealed its use of millions of dollars in tax-exempt teachers' dues and fees for political activities, primarily for Democratic candidates and causes."[10] It is not the intent of this book, however, to delve deeply into their underlying agendas and political purposes--such articles and books already exist in abundance. The NEA's political stance is primarily of interest here because of their attitudes toward and actions against the home schooling movement.

Finally, for those who may require even more evidence for my assertions regarding the political leanings of this powerful and vocal organization, perhaps the following excerpts from an article entitled "NEA Shows Intolerance in Convention Debates" (in which we are given an often appalling glimpse into an actual NEA convention) will help to prove my point:

> "The 1998 NEA convention, like past conventions, was filled with contrasts. Before the debate on the Principles of Unity, President Robert Chase and Vice President Reg Weaver reminded the delegates to be courteous, respectful, and orderly. They were, until the floor discussions included proposed amendments to some long-standing NEA resolutions and several new business items.
>
> It seems that Bob Chase was one of only a few at the convention committed to improving education and

educational opportunities for all children. When a delegate expressed his hope that the Representative Assembly would accept an amendment to an existing NEA resolution censuring home schooling, several unionists loudly proclaimed their opposition and defeated the proposal. Chase was visibly appalled by the exchanges.

Tolerance, acceptance, and open-mindedness are encouraged within the NEA--especially as these ideals relate to gays, lesbians, bisexuals, and transsexuals. However, tolerance did not extend to Christian values. During the debate of an NEA resolution, another delegate expressed concern about the content of *It's Elementary*.

It's Elementary is a lesbian-produced video used to train public school teachers to address and celebrate homosexuality with elementary students beginning at the Kindergarten level. Again, the delegate's concerns were ridiculed by members of the extensive gay and lesbian community within the NEA.

Nor did the majority of the delegates agree to change NEA's Human Rights resolution to reject its present pro-abortion position, although teachers from Ohio, Illinois, New York, and Oklahoma voiced objections on five different occasions. Upon questioning, one delegate received a 'no limits' response to when NEA stops its abortion support during the nine months of pregnancy.
....
Clearly, the union's tolerance of free enterprise and free speech is limited."[11]

Conclusions

So, in the final analysis, the strong animosity of the NEA toward the home school population is really very easy to understand. The success of the home schooling movement has undercut the NEA's ongoing quest for professional respect, control, and money—three very basic and fundamental aspects of any profession's existence. And, as if to add insult to injury, home schoolers are, for the most part, on the opposite side of the "political fence."

Let me close this chapter by reiterating my respect for the teaching profession as a whole. I am very cognizant of the fact that there are many, many public school teachers who do not subscribe to the tenets and beliefs espoused by the NEA. Unfortunately, (as we saw in the excerpts from the convention) their voices are *not* the ones being heard.

We should not be surprised at the ferocity of the NEA's attacks against the home schooling movement. If they are so strident and virulent in their exchanges with disagreeing members of their own association, how can we expect them to be more civil and reasonable in their interactions with others outside the NEA with whom they so violently disagree?

Finally, it must be remembered that the NEA's opposition is *not* based on any educational research. Rather, it would seem to be based primarily on the four elements detailed earlier (i.e., professional pride, control, money, and politics). Happily, the abundant research on home schooling (see Chapter III) favors the home schooling family in terms of both academic and socialization issues.

Endnotes - Chapter IV

[1] NEA 2000-2001 Resolutions; B-68 Home Schooling. Available online at: http:www.nea.org/resolutions/00/00b-68.html (retrieved 3/5/02).

[2] Schlafly, P. (1999, August). Decoding the NEA resolutions. *The Phyllis Schlafly Report, 33* (1). Available online at: http://www.eagleforum.org/psr/1999/aug99.html (retrieved 1/30/02).

[3] Foster, J. (2000, Sept. 11). *NEA vs. Home Schools: Union Opposes Nearly Every Aspect of Parent-Directed Education.* Available online at: www.childrenfirstamerica.org/DailyNews/00Sep/0911003.html (retrieved 1/30/02).

[4] Foster, J. (2000, Sept. 11). *NEA vs. Home Schools: Union Opposes Nearly Every Aspect of Parent-Directed Education.* Available online at: www.childrenfirstamerica.org/DailyNews/00Sep/0911003.html (retrieved 1/30/02)

[5] National Center for Policy Analysis (2000). *Education: A First Step Toward Outlawing Home Schooling in California?* Available online at: http://www.ncpa.org/pi/edu/pd062000b.html (retrieved 1/30/02).

[6] National Center for Policy Analysis (2000). *Education: A First Step Toward Outlawing Home Schooling in California?* Available online at: http://www.ncpa.org/pi/edu/pd062000b.html (retrieved 1/30/02).

[7] (pp. 38-39). Mayberry, M., Knowles, J.G., Ray, B., & Marlow, S. (1995). Home schooling: Parents as educators. Thousand Oaks, CA: Corwin.

[8] (p. 31). Ray, B.D. (1997). Strengths of their own: Home schoolers across America. Salem, OR: NHERI.

[9] McDowell, S.A. (2000). *The "push and pull" of house schooling in the larger society: Using an epidemiological lens to study an educational phenomenon.* Paper presented at the annual meeting of the American Educational Research Association (AERA),

New Orleans. (ERIC Document Reproduction Service No. ED 444 228)

[10] Sorokin, E. (2002, April 23). Complaint accuses NEA of misusing funds to aid DNC. *The Washington Times.* Available online at: http://asp.washtimes.com/printarticle.asp?action=print&ArticleID=20020423-317848 (retrieved 4/24/02).

[11] Education Policy Institute. (1998, July). NEA shows intolerance in convention debates. *Education Exchange, 2* (7). Available online at: http://www.educationpolicy.org/newsletter/EEJul98.htm (retrieved 1/30/02).

Chapter V

Conclusion: This Question Can Be Put to Rest

Let's consider all the elements pertaining to the question of socialization in home schooling that we've examined thus far, and then determine what our conclusion concerning this question should logically and reasonably be.

First, we looked at the question itself. What does the word "socialization" actually mean, and what does the asker of the question imply when he/she asks it? Obviously, the same question does not necessarily hold the same meaning for every person who asks it. Becoming aware of the many and varied meanings possible behind the question helped, hopefully, to lay a proper foundation for a detailed examination of appropriate answers.

Second, we heard from home schoolers themselves. How they respond to and deal with this persistent and often irritating question sheds a great deal of light on the issue itself. Responding sometimes in frustration, sometimes in exasperation, and sometimes with humor, it becomes abundantly clear that the home schooling population as a whole does *not* view socialization as a problematic issue.

Third, we examined the educational research – the element that carries the most weight in legal and legislative matters. Happily, as we have seen, the research indicates that, at best, home schooled children are better socialized than their conventionally schooled counterparts, and, at worst, they are at least as well socialized as their conventionally schooled counterparts.

Fourth, we considered what a strong opponent of the home schooling movement, the National Education Association, had to say. As they have absolutely no research at their disposal to back up their misgivings about home schooling as a viable educational alternative, we explored possible reasons for their negative stance.

Finally, in considering all of these many elements, what conclusion may be safe and sensibly drawn? It may be summed up in a paragraph as follows:

For the vast majority of home schooled children, socialization is not a problematic issue. Indeed, some parents – when considering home schooling as an educational choice – decide to home school their children *because* of the socialization opportunities that home schooling provides. Finally, the research solidly indicates that home schooled children are either better socialized than conventionally schooled children, or at least as well socialized as conventionally schooled children.

How Do You Answer the Question?

How any one home schooler chooses to respond to "But what about socialization?" is, of course, a very personal issue. It depends not only upon the home schooler himself or herself, but upon the situation and the asker of the question. Is the person asking an acquaintance with an arrogant or argumentative attitude, or a family member who is genuinely concerned? Should the answer be brief and to the point, or more comprehensive and detailed? Obviously, each circumstance requires a slightly different approach. Hopefully, the information provided in the preceding chapters will provide more than enough solid ammunition for an appropriate and intelligent response to this persistent question.

For example, when someone asks (in regard to the decision to home school) "But what about socialization?,"a quick, terse retort may be in order, such as:

"According to the research, socialization is not a problem."

For those times when a more detailed response is called for, the following might constitute a suitable reply:

"According to the research, home schooled children are either *better* socialized than conventionally schooled children, or they're at least *as well* socialized as conventionally schooled children. So, socialization is simply not a problem."

Dr. Brian Ray (President, NHERI) suggests yet another alternative for dealing with the question. As he explains, the home schooler "might be able to engage the questioner in a thoughtful and philosophical discussion, asking, 'What do you *mean* by socialization?.' The home schooler could then go on to explain about . . . what the research has shown."

Regardless of the manner in which home schooling parents and children choose to respond to this ever-present and sometimes annoying question, however, the encouraging fact remains that there exists a solid body of research on this issue, and that the findings of said research are positive. In conclusion, then, this question *can* be put to rest.

A Special Message From the Author to Home Schoolers

Clearly -- given the existence of this book, and the very important point that it proves—research is essential to the well being of the home schooling movement. It is research such as that presented in this book that oftentimes stands between the home schooling family and highly unfavorable legal and/or legislative decisions.   And yet, to my great disappointment and even greater surprise, some home schoolers have argued in home schooling publications that *all* cooperation with researchers should cease.

I believe that such an attitude, and any corresponding action, is very much like "throwing the baby out with the baby water." Of course home schoolers should be careful and wise when agreeing to participate in any study. And, if for any reason the process becomes uncomfortable or the home schooler becomes wary of the researcher's motives, the home schooler should simply withdraw from the study as quickly as possible. All researchers are aware of the possibility that a participant might choose to withdraw for some reason or another. It's not a problem.

But please don't decide *not* to participate in a study because of an inherent suspicion of all researchers. Research is an essential and critical element of home school legal defense. Why else would the Home School Legal Defense Association (HSLDA) choose to fund home schooling research?[1]

In the final analysis, however, I believe that Michael Farris (Founder of HSLDA, and founder and President of Patrick Henry College) said it best. Farris and I were among the presenters at a symposium on "The Past, Present, and Probable Future of Home Schooling" at the 1999 meeting of the American Education Research Association. The format of the symposium allowed for the presentation of several research papers, followed by questions from the audience. Interestingly enough, almost all of the papers presented involved statistical analysis.

Farris, who was the last to speak, concluded his presentation and asked for questions from the audience. He gave a swift and unforgettable response to the following question:

"Why do you home school researchers always keep throwing statistics at us?"

Without missing a beat, Michael Farris replied,

"You stop throwing home schoolers in jail, and we'll stop throwing statistics at you."

That was, and still is, the best argument for home schooling research that I've ever heard.

Endnote – Chapter V

1 Rudner, L. M. (1999). Scholastic achievement and demographic characteristics of homes school students in 1998. *Education Policy Analysis Archives, 7* (8) [electronic journal], available online at: http://epaa.asu.edu/epaa/v7n8

Appendix

My own small contribution to original home schooling socialization research was first published in the *Arizona Home Education Journal*, March-April 1999, and is presented in an edited and abbreviated version in this Appendix. Although this research study doesn't add anything entirely new and unexpected to the socialization research, it is helpful in that it serves to reinforce the foundational premise that socialization is *not* perceived as a problem in the home schooling community.

Arizona Home Schooling Families and the Question of Socialization: A Quantitative Study

Introduction

"But what about socialization?" This is a question directed–either innocently or accusingly–to practically every home schooling family at one time or another. As Michael Farris (1997) points out, "Every home schooler would be rich if a $1 fee were imposed on those who ask, 'What about socialization?'"(p. 67).

According to Ray E. Ballmann (1995), the concern behind this frequently asked question is based on "a common misconception. Popular opinion assumes that children need to be around others their own age extensively to be properly socialized" (p. 185). Ballman goes on to note that

> there are two types of socialization, positive and negative. Positive sociability builds responsibility,

cooperation, kindness, fidelity, love, and bilateral trust. It molds a good self-image that delights in putting others first. Negative sociability is the result of coerced age-segregation and builds rivalry, contention, selfishness, peer-dependence, criticism, and derision. It molds a poor self-esteem that responds quickly to peer pressure. (p. 185)

This particular understanding of the socialization issue is echoed by many home schooling parents. As one home schooling mother explained in a recent research study, "There's good and bad socialization . . . kids who run with a gang are socialized. But that's not good socialization" (McDowell, 1998, p. 144).

Clearly, then, what home schooling parents desire for their children is not just socialization in and of itself and for its own sake, but good socialization. It is the purpose of this article to report the results of a research study that looked at this very area of the home schooling experience. To that end, the results of the study are examined and presented in terms of the (a) statement of the research objective, (b) research methodology, (c) results, and (d) conclusions.

Statement of the Research Objective

The purpose of this research study was to determine the perceptions of Arizona home schooling parents as to the issue of socialization, specifically in terms of the following six research questions:

(a) How often were home schooling parents asked about socialization when they first began home schooling?

(b) How are these home schooling parents currently asked about socialization?

(c) What are home schooling parents' perceptions concerning their children's opportunities to interact with other children and adults?

(d) What are home schooling parents' perceptions regarding their children's socialization as compared to the socialization of children attending public schools?

(e) Where do their home schooled children get the majority of their socialization?

(f) What socialization opportunities and/or interactions do home schooling parents consider to be the most important to their children's well being?

Research Methodology

In this section, the research methodology utilized for this research study will be discussed. Specifically, the unit of analysis, the sampling method, and data collection will be examined in appropriate detail.

The Unit of Analysis

The unit of analysis for this research study is the Arizona home schooling parent.

The Sampling Method

As it was virtually impossible (or at least extremely difficult) to obtain the names of all the home schooling families in the state of Arizona, the use of a probability sample–in which each subject has an equal chance of being selected for study–was scarcely feasible. As a result, a non-probability sample was employed. This non-probability sample was of the convenience variety, in that the subjects were comprised of volunteers attending a home schooling curriculum fair. The bias inherent in (a) the self-selection process, and (b) the fact that the population of home schoolers surveyed was composed of only those home schooling parents who chose to attend the Arizona Home Education Convention and Curriculum Fair, will be examined at a later point.

Data Collection

The survey. With the exceptions of Section I (generalized questions about the respondent and his/her experiences with the socialization issue) and Section III (comparisons of respondent's children with non-home schooled children), this survey utilized a Likert-type format, with participants asked to respond to statements by choosing "Frequently," "Sometimes," "Rarely," and "Never" in the first half of the section, and "Very Important, "Somewhat Important," and "Not Really Important" in the second half. The survey is composed of 6 close-ended questions in Section 1, 12 close-ended questions in Section II, and 2 open-ended questions in Section III.

Number of subjects. The researcher handed out a total of 100 surveys–all of which had an attached explanatory letter and a pre-addressed, stamped envelope. Two of the surveys were returned to the researcher prior to the close of the curriculum fair, and 36 were returned by mail to the researcher. Of the 38 surveys, one lacked responses to 35% of the questions, and was thus deemed unsuitable for inclusion. As a result, the final completed sample was made up of 37 completed surveys.

Results

In this section, the methods for data analysis will be presented, along with an examination of the data in light of the guiding research questions.

Analysis of the Data

The data were analyzed using the Statistical Packages for the Social Sciences (1997) computer program. Simple statistics were used to describe participant response in both Sections I and II.

The Research Questions

The research questions guiding this particular research project, and the answers gleaned from the analysis of the data concerning these questions, are detailed in this section. It should be noted at this point that–although it is not one of the six primary research questions–the participant response concerning the number of years engaged in home schooling is of some interest. Analysis of the data revealed that 13.5% of the participants had home schooled for less than 1 year, 37.8% had home schooled for 2 - 4 years, and 48% had been home schooling for 5 or more years.

Research question #1: How often were home schooling parents asked about socialization when they first began home schooling?

The majority of the respondents (67.6%) indicated that they had been asked frequently, 24.3% indicated that they were sometimes asked, 5.4% noted that they were rarely asked, and 2.7% responded that they has never been asked about the issue of socialization.

Research question #2: How often are home schooling parents currently asked about socialization?

Data analysis revealed that 29.8% of the respondents indicated that they were asked frequently, 48.6% noted that they were asked sometimes, and 21.6% indicated that, currently, they were rarely asked about socialization.

Research questions #3: What are home schooling parents' perceptions regarding their children's opportunities to interact with other children and adults?

The majority of parents (78.4%) responded that their children had plenty of opportunities, while 21.6% indicated that their children had adequate opportunities.

Research question #4: What are the perceptions of home schooling parents concerning their children's socialization as compared to the socialization of children attending public schools?

Not surprisingly, 73.0% responded that their children were "better socialized" than children attending public schools. A much smaller percentage (24.3%) indicated that their children were "as well socialized," and a total of 2.7% did not respond to the question.

Research question #5: Where do home schooling parents believe that their children obtain the majority of their socialization?

Participants were asked to rate their children's participation in certain activities utilizing a range of 1.00 ("Frequently") to 4.00 ("Never"). According to respondents, the area in which their children receive their primary socialization is "the family unit" (Mean = 1.054). The second and third areas, respectively, were the "church and church-related activities" (Mean = 1.162), and "interacting with home-schooled friends" (Mean = 1.459). The fourth, fifth, and sixth ranked areas of participation included "home schooling groups" (Mean = 1.891), "interacting with public-schooled friends" (Mean = 1.945), and "Boy Scouts/Girl Scouts, sports groups, and other similar organizations" (Mean = 1.972). (These results are detailed in Table 1.)

Table 1

Means and Standard Deviations for Research Question Five:
Where Do Children Obtain Their Socialization?

Item	Mean	SD
The family unit.	1.054	.3288
Church and church-related activities.	1.162	.3737
Interacting with home-schooled friends.	1.459	.6053
Home schooling groups.	1.891	.8751
Interacting with public-schooled friends.	1.945	.8802
Boy Scouts/Girl Scouts, sports, and other organizations.	1.972	.97

Research question #6: What socialization opportunities/ interactions do home schooling parents consider the most important to their children's well being?

Participants were asked to rate the importance of their children's participation in certain activities utilizing a range of 1.00 ("very important") to 4.00 ("not at all important"). Participants indicated the fundamental importance of the "family unit" with a unanimous response of "very important" (Mean = 1.00). The second most important area was found to be the "church and church-related activities" (Mean = 1.135), and "interacting with home-schooled friends" was judged third in importance (Mean = 1.648). Those items deemed of lesser importance were, respectively, "home schooling groups" (Mean = 1.756), "Boy Scouts/Girl Scouts, sports groups, and other similar organizations" (Mean = 2.027), and "public-schooled friends" (Mean = 2.243). (Table 2 details these results.)

Table 2

Means and Standard Deviations for Research Question Six: What Socialization Opportunities Do Home Schooling Parents Consider the Most Important to Their Children's Well Being?

Item	Mean	SD
The family unit.	1.000	.0000
Church and church-related activities.	1.135	.3466
Interacting with home-schooled friends.	1.648	.5877
Home schooling groups.	1.756	.5965
Boy Scouts/Girl Scouts, sports, and other organizations.	2.027	.7260
Interacting with public-schooled friends.	2.2432	.6414

Limitations of the Study

The use of a non-probability convenience sampling design– and the resulting respondent bias and lack of generalizability to a larger population – is the primary limitation of this research study. Respondent bias – in that the respondents were volunteering to participate in the survey and were therefore self-selected – is yet another limitation of the study.

Conclusions

What are the perceptions of Arizona home schooling parents as to the issue of socialization? They are, according to the results of this survey, generally quite favorable. The majority of participants indicated that they (a) had, indeed, been asked frequently about the issue of socialization when they first began home schooling; (b) are currently asked about socialization "sometimes"; (c) perceive their children to have plenty of opportunity to interact with other children and adults; (d) perceive their children to be better socialized than children attending public schools; (e) believe that their children get their primary socialization from (in order of participation) the family unit, the church and church-related activities, interaction with home-schooled friends, home schooling groups, interaction with public-schooled friends, and Boy Scouts/Girl Scouts/Similar Organizations; and (f) believe the most important socialization opportunities/ interactions for their children to be (in order of importance) the family unit, the church and church-related activities, interaction with home-schooled friends, home school groups, Boy Scouts/Girl Scouts/Similar Organizations, and public-schooled friends.

As was noted earlier, the generalizability of this particular survey instrument is limited in the extreme. Even so, it is clear from these results that the majority of the participants consider the family and the church to be of primary importance to the social well being of their children. The majority of respondents also consider their children to be better socialized than those children attending public schools.

It is possible, in the final analysis, to consider the issue of socialization with both humor and practicality. For instance, it is altogether possible that the participants in this survey would agree wholeheartedly with Thomas Lewis's (President of AFHE) description of his own children's socialization, when he explained that he and his wife measure their children's socialization by the number of miles on their car's speedometer. "Last year," Lewis noted, "my kids got 20,000 miles worth of socialization!" Surely many home schooling parents could both sympathize and empathize with this last statement.

References

Ballmann, R.E. (1995). *The how and why of home schooling* (2nd ed.). Wheaton, IL: Crossway Books.

Farris, M. (1997). *The future of home schooling: A new direction for home education.* Washington, DC: Regnery.

McDowell, S.A. (1998). *Home sweet school: The perceived impact of home schooling on the family in general and the mother-teacher in particular.* Unpublished doctoral dissertation, Peabody College of Vanderbilt University, Nashville, TN.

Suggested Bibliography

Ballman, R. E. (1987). *The how and why of home schooling* (2nd ed.). Wheaton, IL: Crossway Books.

Bell, D. (1997). *The ultimate guide to homeschooling.* Nashville, TN: Thomas Nelson.

Blumenfeld, S. L. (1998). *Homeschooling: A parents guide to teaching children.* Secaucus, NJ: Citadel Press.

Card, S., & Card, M. (1997). *The homeschool journey.* Eugene, OR: Harvest House.

Colfax, D., & Colfax, M. (1988). *Homeschooling for excellence.* New York: Warner Books.

Farris, M. (1997). *The future of home schooling: A new direction for Christian home education.* Washington, DC: Regnery.

Gorder, C. (1985). *Home schools: An alternative.* Columbus, OH: Blue Bird.

Griffith, M. (1997). *The homeschooling handbook.* Rocklin, CA: Prima.

Guterson, D. (1992). *Family matters: Why homeschooling makes sense.* New York: Harcourt Brace.

Holt, J. (1981). *Teach your own: A hopeful path for education.* New York: Delacorte Press/Seymour Lawrence.

Llewellyn, G. (Ed.). *Real lives: Eleven teenagers who don't go to school.* Eugene, OR: Lowry House.

Mayberry, M., Knowles, J. G., Ray, B. D., & Marlow, S. (1995). *Home schooling: Parents as educators.* Thousand Oaks, CA: Corwin Press.

Moore, R., & Moore, D. (1994). *The successful homeschool family handbook: A creative and stress-free approach to homeschooling.* Nashville, TN: Thomas Nelson.

Pagnoni, M. (1984). *The complete home educator: A comprehensive guide to modern home-teaching.* New York: Larson.

Pedersen, A., & O'Mara, P. (Eds.). (1990). *Schooling at home: Parents, kids, and learning.* Santa Fe, NM: John Muir Publications/Mothering Magazine.

Ray, B. D. (1997). *Strengths of their own – Home Schoolers across America: Academic achievement, family characteristics, and longitudinal traits.* Salem, OR: National Home Education Research Institute.

Ray, B. D. (1999). *Home schooling on the threshold: A survey of research at the dawn of the new millennium.* Salem, OR: National Home Education Research Institute.

Ray, B. D. (2002). *A quick reference worldwide guide to home-schooling: Facts and stats on the benefits of home school, 2002, 2003.* Nashville, TN: Broadman & Holman.

Ray, B. D. (2002). *Home centered learning annotated bibliography* (11th ed.). Salem, OR: NHERI.

Rudner, L. M. (1999). Scholastic achievement and demographic characteristics of homes school students in 1998. *Education Policy Analysis Archives, 7* (8) [electronic journal], available online at: http://epaa.asu.edu/epaa/v7n8

Sheffer, S. (1995). *A sense of self: Listening to homeschooled adolescent girls.* Portsmouth, NH: Heinemann.